STRATEGY AND THE NATIONAL SECURITY PROFESSIONAL

STRATEGY AND THE NATIONAL SECURITY PROFESSIONAL

STRATEGIC THINKING AND STRATEGY FORMULATION IN THE 21ST CENTURY

Harry R. Yarger

PRAEGER SECURITY INTERNATIONAL
Westport, Connecticut • London

Library of Congress Cataloging-in-Publication Data

Yarger, Harry R. (Harry Richard)
    Strategy and the national security professional : strategic thinking and strategy
formulation in the 21st century / Harry R. Yarger.
        p.   cm.
    Includes bibliographical references and index.
    ISBN-13: 978-0-313-34849-5 (alk. paper)
    1. Strategy.   2. National security—United States—21st century.
3. United States—Military policy. I. Title.
    U162.Y3183   2008
    355'.0335—dc22   2008009957

British Library Cataloguing in Publication Data is available.

Library of Congress Catalog Card Number: 2008009957
ISBN-13: 978-0-313-34849-5

First published in 2008

Praeger Security International, 88 Post Road West, Westport, CT 06881
An imprint of Greenwood Publishing Group, Inc.
www.praeger.com

Printed in the United States of America

The paper used in this book complies with the
Permanent Paper Standard issued by the National
Information Standards Organization (Z39.48–1984).

10 9 8 7 6 5 4 3 2 1

Contents

Preface

This book focuses on strategic theory, strategic thinking, and strategy formulation. In the process it seeks to inform policy formulation and place planning in the proper context in relation to policy and strategy. Its focus is on strategy at the highest levels of the nation-state and is applicable to grand strategy, national security strategy, national military strategy, other national-level strategies, and regional or theater strategy. It does not propose a specific strategy for the United States; rather, it provides theory and a framework for considering and formulating all state strategy. It is an examination of theory, exploring those aspects of strategy that appear to have universal application. It is written specifically to expose senior leaders, strategists, and other members of the national security community to the vocabulary, ideas, and concepts that make strategy a discipline so that a common framework exists for developing and debating different policy and strategic perspectives in regard to the trends, issues, opportunities, and threats confronting the United States as a nation-state in the twenty-first century.

Few in the United States understand the role and theory of strategy, and fewer still can actually formulate it. Yet, the word "strategy" pervades American conversation and our media. Americans tend to use strategy as an interchangeable term for a plan, concept, course of action, or "vision" at the personal, organizational, and state levels. Such casual use of the term to describe nothing more than "what we would like to do next" is inappropriate and belies the complexity of true strategy formulation and strategic thinking. It reduces strategy to just a good idea without the necessary underlying theory, depth of thought, or careful formulation required for success. It also leads to confusion among policy, strategy, and planning by confining strategic possibilities to near-term political aspirations, planning processes, and inappropriate and confining details. At the same time it limits the flexibility of strategic thought and sets inappropriately detailed expectations of outcomes. As a result of not properly formulating and articulating coherent strategy, the natural interaction in the strategic environment is mistaken for strategic failure and national will can be lost. New "plans" posing as strategy are rushed forward and national expectations are recocked for the next failure.

This book is not a research book in a classic sense. It is intended to present a coherent picture of the strategic environment and the strategic thinking required to formulate and implement policy and strategy. As such it borrows freely from the ideas and concepts of others: some of whom have historical or global recognition and others who toiled namelessly as faculty members and students at various military senior service colleges. I apologize to all for those instances wherein I may have misrepresented their ideas or paraphrased too closely without proper recognition in my quest for a synthesis of thought that might qualify as pure theory. I also apologize to readers for the frequent redundancy and complexity of my work—but strategy is a complex subject that is better understood when examined from different perspectives. In the same light I have used examples very sparingly and reluctantly, only as a means to indicate the path of my thinking. To do more would beg for the illustration to be challenged instead of the thought or suggest the direct application of the "lessons" of the example to similar circumstances. A theory of strategy is neither a simple checklist nor a cookbook solution. It is a way to understand how you might develop a perspective and approach for defining and selecting alternative choices in an increasingly complex and rapidly changing world—focusing on "how to think" as opposed to "what to think"—and articulating your choices in ways that can be understood and implemented. Strategy is neither simple nor easy, but the good strategist seeks to express the logic of strategy in the simplest, clearest terms.

1

Introduction

Like politics, strategy is the art of the possible; but few can discern what is possible.[1]

—Williamson Murray and Mark Grimsley

The twenty-first century security environment is both promising for and threatening to the national security interests of the nation-state. Indeed, some have argued that the epoch of the nation-state is at an end. This judgment is obviously premature, since nationalism remains a source of both conflict and stability in the current world order.[2] What is true is that the bipolar stability in world order sustained by the Cold War balance of power has ended and, since the collapse of the Soviet Union, the international order has been seeking a new balance of acceptable stability. Policymakers and professionals within governmental departments and agencies, both civilian and military, who are responsible for protecting and advancing the interests of the United States, are confronted with a strategic environment that is much more volatile, uncertain, complex, and ambiguous than that faced by their twentieth century predecessors. In large part, the success of their predecessors' strategy has compounded the current challenge by creating and unleashing the loosely defined phenomenon of "globalism."[3] This new strategic environment requires a renaissance in strategic thinking for the United States to continue to lead in the twenty-first century.

Globalism means different things to different constituencies, but what it clearly does not mean is a period of international peace and stability. If the liberal capitalistic world order the United States and its allies promoted to defeat communism created great opportunity to realize individual and national potential in the twenty-first century, it also created the environment for individuals, organizations, and states to exploit that opportunity for their own purposes. Consequently, the United States finds itself challenged with new threats and the resurgence of old ones. Religious terrorism, international criminal cartels, resurgent nationalism, emboldened adversaries, and contrarian allies and friends all characterize this new era. In effect, the current strategic environment has not found an acceptable new stability for a twenty-first century world order. The problem for the United States is compounded by the fact that the domestic consensus that sustained national unity and identity in the Cold War has been shattered by success and the ensuing domestic opportunism in politics, business, and individual pursuits. The strategic dilemma in which the United States finds itself today is greater than it has ever been in our history—it owns the twenty-first century but is strategically clueless as to what to do with it. Paradoxically, at the time it is most needed, our leaders appear increasingly inept at thinking strategically, and the "sound bite" has replaced the national debate on policy and strategy. The dilemma is so evident that it appears to be nothing less than a systemic failure in the policy and strategy formulation processes throughout the government.

The strategic pause by the United States following the Cold War has become somewhat of a strategic embarrassment as the United States has failed to live up to the promise of its ideals. Neither the executive branch nor the Congress has provided a unifying vision that articulates and inspires the American people for their role in this new century. Neither has produced effective leadership that can articulate clear and compelling policies or a grand strategy and implementing strategies that will shape a more favorable future for Americans and ensure their security. Much of the policy and strategy that has been pursued or advocated has fallen short of its aims and alienated most of the rest of the international community, while further fragmenting domestic support. Great opportunities for a more secure future in a U.S.-inspired international order have been squandered and new adversaries have emerged since the collapse of the Berlin Wall. It is as if the political leadership and national security community as a whole have forgotten what strategic thinking is and how to intelligently debate differences in ideas about policy and strategy. Could it be that the strategic framework that the Cold War created with its relative stability followed by a self-imposed strategic pause has dulled our strategic perspective in how to think about the debate and formulate policy and strategy? Much of the evidence suggests this is the case. As this paragraph is being written in the fall of 2007, the national debate over U.S. involvement in Iraq has been reduced to the number of troops in country as opposed to what U.S. interests are in the region and the consequences of success or failure in creating a stable, democratic Iraq.

In hindsight, it appears our adversaries, real or potential, and many of our Cold War friends took no strategic pause and used the world order the United States produced and secured to gain significant advantages. Islamic extremists have made their bid, calculating that time and international public opinion are on their side. Who can say what Russia will choose to be in the long term? China may or may not emerge as a twenty-first century military peer threat. Her immersion into the world economy is a positive step for peaceful integration, but she has gained significant economic advantages over the United States around the world and is modernizing military forces. Much of Europe has plotted a different political course in the Middle East than that of the United States, serving their proprietary interests and allowing America to shoulder the animosity inherent in sustaining stability in the region. The rise of civil society has empowered non-state actors and challenged ideas of state behavior and global leadership. Clearly, the United States can no longer rely on an automatic deference to its interests previously enjoyed as the leader of the free world. Today, if we are to lead in the world and shape a free future, we must ensure that we pursue policies and strategies that keep our national powers strong and build trust internationally in both our desire and ability to create a better future for all. It is in this promise that U.S. national security and a better future for Americans lies. Political leadership, and those who engage in the formulation and debate over national security policy and strategy, must reengage in vigorous strategic thinking and informed debate on how to best do this.

Such a vigorous debate and subsequent successful policy and strategy are possible only if those who are in power, the national security professionals who support them, the national media who over watch them, and an informed public prepare themselves to participate. At the heart of such preparation is learning how to think strategically and how to formulate effective policy and strategy. Learning is complicated because there is no comprehensive theory of strategy to provide shared concepts and vocabulary for a legitimate intellectual discussion. Participants who now try to engage in such debate are confused by what distinguishes policy, strategy, and planning. Mixing the three without understanding the distinctions, policymakers, strategists, and national security professionals at all levels have produced neither good policy nor good strategy. Consequently, the planning function has been problematic and largely inadequate for the circumstances those on the frontline of national engagement find themselves in. The situation has been further compounded by a national media that is equally confused and, in turn, the media often misleads an over reactive public. The resulting domestic politics further compounds the difficulty in achieving a proper debate and a national consensus to move the nation forward. It is a crisis of strategic thinking among the entire national security community.

In this book the author first distinguishes among policy, strategy, and planning. He then offers a theory of strategy and insights on strategic thinking that promote better policy and strategy formulation, and subsequently more appropriate planning. In doing this, a heavy reliance is placed on military theorists for the simple reason that these theorists have done the most work in regard to a theory of strategy. However, strategy is not limited to the military domain and this should be evident to the reader as he considers the concepts and vocabulary offered here. National security is about much more than the use of the military and requires the development and application of all the nation's elements of power. Furthermore, it always has internal as well as external components that complicate its realization. In simplistic terms, strategy at all levels is defined as the calculation of objectives, concepts, and resources within acceptable bounds of risk to create more favorable outcomes than might otherwise exist by chance or at the hands of others. Strategy is formally defined in U.S. military Joint Publication 1-02 as: "A prudent idea or set of ideas for employing the instruments of national power in a synchronized and integrated fashion to achieve theater, national and/or multinational objectives."[4] Both of these definitions are useful but neither fully conveys the role and complexity of strategic thought.

Strategy can be better understood as the *art* and *science* of developing and using the political, economic, socio-psychological, and military powers of the state in accordance with policy guidance to create effects and set conditions that protect or advance national interests relative to other states, actors, or circumstances. Strategy seeks a synergy and symmetry of objectives, concepts, and resources to increase the probability of policy success and the favorable consequences that follow from that success. It is a process that seeks to apply a degree of rationality and linearity to circumstances that may or may not be either. Strategy though complex accomplishes this by expressing its logic in rational, linear terms—simply identified as ends, ways, and means. Policy can be best understood as political guidance in regard to the end-state sought by strategy, but such guidance can also apply to the specific ends, ways, and means of strategy. In fact, some would argue that strategy at the political level is policy, but for reasons that will become evident this text takes a different view.

Strategy formulation is both an *art* and a *science*. Viewed as an art, strategy formulation can be interpreted as the realm of rare genius where talented leaders intuitively arrive at grand solutions to complex issues of foreign policy and war. True genius cannot be denied, but few states in today's dynamic environment can afford to await the arrival of the proverbial genius. Comfort can be found for the majority of practising national security professionals in the fact that strategy is also a science. It suggests that strategy formulation can be observed, theorized about, and perhaps improved in its application through study and experience. Indeed, over time numerous authorities, such as Sun Tzu, Carl von Clausewitz, and Colin Gray, have acknowledged the essence of art and genius in strategy while providing observations and theoretical constructs that help us better understand the practice of strategy formulation.[5] Understanding the nature of the strategic environment and a theory of strategy allows us to grasp and work with its complexity by understanding its logic. A theory of strategy provides: essential terminology and definitions; explanations of the underlying assumptions and premises; substantive propositions translated into testable hypotheses; and methods that can be used to test the hypotheses and modify the theory as appropriate.[6]

Theory's value lies not in a prescription for success but in how it helps us expand and discipline our thinking. As Clausewitz reminds us, theory should be for study, not doctrine:

> Theory then becomes a guide to anyone who wants to learn about war from books; it will light his way, ease his progress, training his judgment, and help him to avoid pitfalls.... Theory exists so that one need not start afresh each time sorting out the material and plowing through it, but will find it ready to hand and in good order. It is meant to educate the mind of the future commander....[7]

A theory of strategy educates the strategist and policymaker's minds. It helps discipline the national security professional's thinking in order to deal with the complexity and volatility of the strategic environment and the changes and continuities, issues, opportunities, and threats inherent to it. It encourages us to rethink our own assumptions and prejudices, but it also encourages us to consider the possible assumptions and prejudices of our adversaries and other actors. Strategic theory opens the mind of all to all the possibilities and forces at play, prompting us to consider the costs and risks of our decisions and weigh the consequences of those of our adversaries, allies, and others. On another level, theory allows the members of the national security profession and others to communicate intelligently in regard to strategy. It serves as a common frame of reference for the development and evaluation of appropriate policy and strategy and the communication of it to those who must implement it. A theory of strategy also enables the professional to evaluate the merits of a particular policy or strategy and critique it in meaningful terms to policy and decision makers.

With such a notable collection of theorists explaining the science of strategy, why do so many strategies fail to meet the test of reality when executed? The answer is that strategy is far from simple, and strategic thinking is difficult. The theorists got it correct. It is best viewed as both an art and a science. The framework of theory provides a methodological basis for a disciplined thought process to assist the strategist in developing strategy, and it also serves as a guide for others to follow in comprehending, evaluating, and critiquing the merits of a particular strategy. While theory is an important aid for educating the mind, it is not a substitute for the particular "genius" described by Clausewitz. History's great strategists possessed "a very highly developed mental aptitude" combining art and science in an ability to perceive the realities, relationships, and possibilities of their environment, and integrating them successfully in formulating strategy.[8] True genius is rare, and some say that it is no longer applicable in the modern, complex world. It is, they argue, too difficult for a single person—even a genius—to comprehend all the nuances of the modern world, and they propose that strategy is better served by an organizational process. In spite of these views, however, strategies often are linked to individual personalities in the public eye, and some individuals appear to have a particular talent for this art and science.[9] Regardless of whether strategy is derived from individual genius, organizational process, or national debate the ability to think strategically is crucial to those who participate in national security whether a policymaker, strategist, leader, or planner.

CONCLUSION

This text is intended as a single source reference for the political appointee, national security professional, or others who participate in the formulation, evaluation, and execution of policy and strategy or those who study and follow national security debates. Its primary focus is on strategy, but it also argues understanding strategic thinking and strategy formulation contribute to better policymaking. It does not propose a new twenty-first century strategy or focus on critiquing current strategy, but offers a perspective and process for disciplined strategic thought in regard to all strategy. It is comprehensive in its explanation of the nature of the strategic environment, offering a clear and comprehensive theory of strategy, and a practical framework for thinking about this environment and formulating effective policy and strategy. It helps the reader understand the nature of international and domestic aspects of the strategic environment that make strategy formulation and execution so difficult for the nation-state, and particularly within a democracy. It argues that with a proper environmental assessment and appraisal, the key strategic factors can be identified and appropriate policy and strategy can be debated and formulated. The book then instructs the reader on how to develop and clearly articulate the objectives, concepts, and resources in strategy, and how to avoid common errors and pitfalls in strategy formulation. It also provides practical tests for the validity of a particular strategy and how to consider and articulate risk. In a larger sense, what it offers is a conceptual framework for individuals, organizations, and national security communities to understand the nature of the strategic environment and how strategic theory applies in policy and strategy formulation. Its dual function is to serve as summary to remind the experienced practitioner of what he must consider and a primer to instruct the novice of the breadth of what he must reflect on. Its hope is that through a shared framework of theory, concepts, vocabulary, and understanding the national security community can better debate and formulate policy and strategy in the Republic's service.

2

Policy, Strategy, Planning, and Strategic Thinking

But the effects of genius show not so much in novel forms of action as in the ultimate success of the whole. What we should admire is the accurate fulfillment of the unspoken assumptions, the smooth harmony of the whole activity, which only become evident in the final success.[1]

—Clausewitz

Policy, strategy, and planning are all interrelated, but the relationship among them and the purpose and use of policy, strategy, and planning are often misunderstood and misused in the national security environment. All three share the ends, ways, and means paradigm, and all three employ degrees of strategic thinking. However, each is also distinct in its purpose and its application—each has its own mindset. And while there is a hierarchical relationship among policy, strategy, and planning when they are addressing the same areas of concern, there is no theoretical requirement that every policy has a subordinate strategy or that all planning has to be guided by a superior strategy. Policy, strategy, and planning are all legitimate processes in their own right and can occur at any level in the government hierarchy and for any realm of concern. The relationship among the three is dependent on the nature and structural level of the concern, the degree of complexity of the concern, the time parameters, and the foresight and choices of leadership. This chapter offers a simplified overview of the distinctions among the three and of strategic thinking before detailed nuances are developed in later chapters.

Policy at its core is simply guidance. It is the prerogative of leadership at any level to provide guidance on any topic. Hence a leader of any organization can state policy for that organization as long as it does not conflict with the directions or intent of his superiors. National policy is policy with a big "P" approved by the president. It is the result of *a political process and decision*, while strategy and planning by nature *seek to be apolitical and adhere to disciplined intellectual models*—treating policy as a factor, and not participating in the political process. Such "Policy" is national political guidance and must be adhered to by all subordinate policy, strategy, and planning to which it applies. For example, the secretary of state can establish policy for the Department of State, but if later superior national policy or national strategy conflicts with his guidance, he must revise his guidance. Such state policy would also logically be revised to support the intent of national policy as well as eliminate conflicts. State policy would also internalize, where applicable, all national-level strategies approved by the president, seeking to support their intent and avoid conflicting effects within his organization. This subordination to national-level policy and strategy would be true for all executive departments and agencies.

There are formalized processes for the development, coordination, articulation, and dissemination of national policy, but as will be developed later, it does not have to adhere to this process.[2] National policy can be stated with specific ends, ways, and means as fully articulated as those required of strategy, but often it is not, even when it comes through the formal processes. It may be announced as policy objectives or as general guidance such as U.S. policy is to support democratic elections. National policy can also be developed and disseminated less formally as a result of immediate security demands or presidential styles. A more recent national policy can be superior to existing policy, strategy, and planning, but it does not necessarily apply to all or invalidate every part of existing ones. The nature and intent of the policy statement determines that. Thus, policy can require a new strategy, require a modification of an existing strategy, provide more specific guidance to some aspect of the strategy, or apply on a one-time basis to a specific issue and not affect existing strategy beyond that. Strategy is subordinate to political guidance, but strategy can generate clarifying and supporting policy. For example, NSC 68 was a policy document prepared in 1950 that many argue constituted a U.S. grand strategy for the Cold War, possessing all the attributes of strategy in theory. As such, it served successfully as a guiding grand strategy for the Cold War period even though successive presidents adapted its provisions through numerous policies, doctrines, and national security strategies.[3] National policy is superior to strategy because it is political guidance, but context and relevancy determine its applicability and relationship to a particular strategy.

Strategy is a disciplined intellectual process with clearly defined outputs of ends, ways, and means that serve national political purpose and policy in the context of the volatile, uncertain, complex, and ambiguous nature of the strategic environment. It adheres to the logic of strategic theory and a specific disciplined thought process. While much of strategic theory and the strategic thought processes may be equally applicable to national policy formation, strategy differs in its purpose, scope, and time horizon. Strategy is cognizant of political purpose, but it is fundamentally not a political process. Its purpose is to translate political purpose—national purpose, interests, and policy guidance—into strategic effects that shape the strategic environment favorably. It is holistic in its scope and specific in its realm. Strategy is future oriented and problem defining and avoiding, as opposed to problem solving. It does this through a specific appraisal of the strategic environment to determine and select key strategic factors that must be addressed in order to advance state interests successfully. From the synthesis and evaluation of these factors, strategy produces a rational statement of ends, ways, and means that create effects leading to the desired future. In doing this, strategy serves the purpose of policy, ensures flexibility and adaptability, and defines the boundaries for planning.

Planning is a disciplined problem-solving process with clearly defined outputs in terms of ends, ways, and means. Planning seeks to create certainty by accounting for all the pertinent variables in the environment, determining the cause-and-effect relationships among them, and addressing each through the plan's articulation of ends, ways, and means, or the articulation of the plan's sequels and contingencies. Planning can be long term or short term. A long-term 20-year plan is not inconsistent with planning's logic as long as the planning organization has a relatively clear vision of the future and can forecast the problems to be encountered. If this is true, planning has been sufficiently bounded and can set about confronting the problems so the vision can be realized. At the national level, few long-term interests or issues are this simple. Thus, formation of a strategy is necessary to appraise the environment and determine the necessary effects for success, and then articulate appropriate ends, ways, and means that lead to those effects. Planning then is bounded and can set about solving the problem of achieving strategy's ends within the confines of the provided ways and means. It does this by analyzing the problems posed by strategy's ends, ways, and means and developing its own set of detailed, subordinate ends, ways, and means leading to achieving strategy's objectives.

Planning often enjoys a direct relationship with policy. In most crisis and many individual issues at the policy level, the immediate policy objective is essentially one of problem solving. Often, the policy statement solves the resolution of the issues, and it only needs to be implemented through incorporation into existing plans or direct action supported by appropriate planning. An issue's urgency may also require expeditious action that is not covered by existing strategy or plans and authority. Indeed, even when strategy and supporting plans preexist that foresee potential incidents, the U.S. government will do crisis action planning because significant real-world events need to be reassessed in the immediate contemporary context before action is taken. Existing strategy and plans inform this reassessment, and they may be validated or modified based on the real-time assessment. If the event is significant enough, it may require a reevaluation of existing policy, strategy, and plans to see if the change caused by the event invalidates or requires their modification. Planners need to understand strategic theory and thinking so that they can implement policy and strategy. They also need to understand the implications of planning decision recommendations for broader policy goals and strategy when doing crisis-action planning or direct policy-issue planning.

Strategic thinking in the purest sense is the capacity to apply strategic theory in the real world and formulate strategy that successfully advances specific state interests without undue risk of creating negative consequences for the state's other interests. It has aspects of both art and science that enable the possessor to synthesize the volatility, uncertainty, complexity, and ambiguity that characterize the strategic environment, evaluate its unpredictability, and formulate a rational statement of strategy. National security professionals in the policy arena apply strategic thinking in day-to-day policy formulation, but accept that the more difficult and most complex longer-term issues and situations require policy to direct formulation of a strategy. Planners, who translate strategy into specific plans and operations, need to appreciate strategic thinking in order to plan appropriately, adapt where necessary, and recognize what constitutes success or failure.

Theorists in various disciplines help us understand the nature of strategic thinking and the competencies required to think strategically. Strategic theory, as advanced in the next chapter, captures the essence of strategic thought, but understanding and applying it requires the possession or appreciation and use of a number of thinking competencies. In educating senior-level military officers and government officials, the U.S. Army War College focuses on five specific thinking domains that serve as lenses for appraising, evaluating, and addressing the challenges of the strategic environment: critical thinking, systems thinking, thinking in time, ethical thinking, and creative thinking.[4] There are other frameworks for understanding thinking at this level, but all such frameworks act as lenses to discipline the strategist's or national security professional's thought processes, reminding him of the dimensions of the intellect that should be applied to the formulation and execution of policy and strategy. Theory gives us a framework for considering and formulating policy and strategy; strategic thinking applies the framework in such a manner as to yield the best possible policy and strategy. Considering strategic thinking competencies as distinct is useful for purposes of definition and understanding, but strategic thinking is best

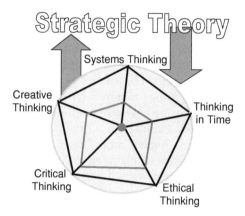

Figure 2.1 Strategic Thinking Competencies.[5]

understood as the integrative and iterative application of these competencies as depicted in Figure 2.1. The strategic thought process as provided later in this text helps demonstrate how this can be done.

Critical thinking as a competency is the ability to deliberately, consciously, and appropriately apply reflective skepticism. It is the purposeful, reflective, and careful evaluation of information in order to improve one's judgment. It requires an open mind that is willing to question and challenge conventional wisdom and one's own point of view. It does this first by clarifying the concern or fully understanding the nature and complexity of the issue and its subcomponents and framing it appropriately so that options in regard to it are not unnecessarily limited. Next is the consideration of different points of view and the self awareness to look beyond one's own egocentric tendencies. Another component in a critical thinking process is to carefully look for and evaluate assumptions about the issue and how the world functions in regard to it. Critical thinking next considers what inferences need to be considered. The critical thinker must be adept at drawing inferences as well as able to see and objectively evaluate inferences that he or others may be proffering. Recognizing the roles and value of points of view, assumptions, and inferences, the critical thinker purposefully evaluates information relative to the issue. In evaluating information the critical thinker actively seeks to avoid cognitive errors by purposefully considering the role of heuristics, biases, and reasoning fallacies in his thinking and that of others. Once information has been appropriately discerned, the critical thinker considers the implications of all he has learned in regard to the issue: facts, points of view, assumptions, inferences, both the short-term and long-term possibilities, and the potential relationships and multiple-ordered effects. From this reflective judgment, intellectual conclusions flow in regard to strategy, ultimately leading to the formulation of ends, ways, and means.

Like all strategic thought, critical thinking is integrative and iterative.[6] Critical thinking in policy and strategy is about depth and breadth in thinking, objectivity, and the quality and applicability of choices.

Systems thinking is another essential competency in strategic thinking. It allows the individual to deal with complex situations that are beyond a cause-and-effect relationship. While whole books have been written about systems thinking, the essence of the competency is the ability to see and think about the whole of any issue or environment rather than just the parts. It sees things in terms of systems in which the parts are interdependent as opposed to simply cause-and-effect relationships. Systems may be simple and predictable or complex and dynamic. The strategic environment is the latter. In strategic thinking the first step is to identify the whole of the system. The second step is to understand and define the behavior or properties of the whole system. This process is one of synthesis as opposed to analysis. The last step is to understand individual aspects of the system in regard to their roles or functions within the whole and the effects of any changes induced on the whole.[7] Systems thinking in policy and strategy is about being able to recognize the nature of the strategic environment: a nature of interdependence, volatility, uncertainty, complexity, and ambiguity.

Creative thinking is the ability to develop new ideas and concepts that identify, explain, and help resolve current or potential issues and situations. Creative thinking is hindered by traditional educational and developmental programs that stress rational and linear thinking and standardize approaches to problem solving and issue resolution. While these have great value in dealing with familiar and routine problems and situations, the nature of the strategic environment often poses open-ended situations in which the nature of the issue, the best means of dealing with it, and the consequences of acting or not acting are unclear. Creative thinking in policy and strategy increases understanding, broadens the possible explanations and alternative choices, and identifies potential opportunities.[8]

Thinking in time is the quality of thought that understands the role of both continuities from the past and the processes of change in the shaping of the future—the ability to see time as a continuous stream. It connects discrete phenomena over time and is able to relate the connections to potential futures and choices for a desired future. Some have described this competency in part as "imagining the future as it may be when it becomes the past—with some intelligible continuity but richly complex and able to surprise." If this can be done, a strategic bridge can be built to the desired future. Thus, it enables the strategist to imagine a realistic future because of his understanding of its sources in the past and alerts him of what kind of and how much care and effort must be taken in shaping a desired future—suggesting what to change and how to go about it.[9] Thinking in time in policy and strategy mitigates uncertainty, complexity, and ambiguity.

Ethical thinking is an important competency in the formulation of policy and strategy. It bears directly on their success. This is especially true for a democracy and in a globalized world. "Ethics essentially prescribes human behavior as being obligatory (what one must do), prohibited (what one must not do) or permissible (what one may do)."[10] Carl von Clausewitz in *On War* noted that theory and, by implication, strategy becomes infinitely more complicated as soon as it touches the realm of moral values. In fact, he argues military activity is directed as much against moral forces as material ones and everyone tries to assess the spirit and temper of their own forces as well as the foes'. His experience recognized that moral forces give life to material capabilities.[11] Ethical thinking as a competency evaluates the "rightness" of a policy or strategy. It gets at the acceptability of policy and strategy, both at home and among other actors, and the effects of strategic behavior and its consequences.[12]

National security professionals serve in many positions. While most are never strategists proper, strategic thinking and an understanding of strategy formulation are desired competencies for most. At the U.S. Army War College three roles for strategists are considered: leader, practitioner, and theorist. These roles have applications across the institutions and agencies of the state. Each of these roles requires distinct skills sets and competencies. The leader provides the necessary vision, inspiration, organizational skills, direction, and personal leadership to enable others to act in a focused and coherent manner. The practitioner thoroughly comprehends the levels of strategy and their relationships and develops specific strategy. He translates broad policy guidance into integrated strategies that lead to policy success. The theorist develops theories and concepts through study and thought, and then he teaches and mentors others. In this model a master of the strategic art is proficient in all three of these roles and may approach Clausewitz's genius.[13] What the three individual roles and the master share is their understanding of strategic theory and its implications for their roles. While some in these roles may possess all the other competencies described above, it is not common and is not required. What is required are strategic-level thinking and an appreciation for theory and the various lenses and the inclusion of those with these capabilities on the policy or strategy formulation team.

Members of the national security community function at different levels or in different roles within the state's and other institutions' organizational hierarchies. All need to understand the formulation of policy and comprehensive strategies and effectively communicate them amongst themselves and with the leadership, the planners, and the people who make up the organizations that implement policy and strategy, and ultimately with the American people. Thus, successful policy and strategy is dependent on the understanding of them by people working in roles other than that of the policymaker or strategist. Admittedly, a larger burden falls on the executive branch of government, but it is equally valid to argue that those members of the national security community who exist in the legislative branch, the press, academia, think tanks, and special interest groups that have constitutional or assumed roles and interests in state policy and strategy also need to comprehend a theory of strategy and need to apply reflective strategic-level thinking when contributing to the intellectual debate. In fact, it could be argued that in the Republic every informed citizen should have some appreciation for the nature of strategy.

CONCLUSION

Policy and strategy give purpose and direction to the state. However, policy is derived through a political process, and strategy is formulated from a disciplined strategic thought process founded in theory and practice. Policy is hierarchically superior to strategy when they address the same interests or issue on the same level or when the strategy is on a subordinate level. Conversely, policy can be subordinate to grand or higher levels of strategy depending on context. Policy, strategy, and planning share the paradigm of ends, ways, and means, but serve different purposes within the state. Planning follows a distinct planning process and may directly support strategy or policy. Policy ideally is formulated from a similar strategic thought process as strategy but, as a political process, it is not required to adhere to either form or substance of theory. Practice in policy varies among administrations and even within administrations. Strategy must adhere to theory, process, and form in its formulation and articulation. Hence a study of strategic theory and practice informs policy formulation, but does not dictate to it.

Thus, policy and strategy provide proactive direction for the state, seeking to maximize positive outcomes and minimize negative consequences, as the state moves through a complex and rapidly changing environment into the future. Strategists and other members of the national security community thoroughly assess the environment and formulate, evaluate, execute, and critique policies and strategies in regard to the choices of objectives, concepts, and resources. In this text the author uses the term strategist somewhat interchangeably with policymaker and national security professional because all require an understanding of the theory of strategy and strategic thinking to perform well, but it is the strategist who is most accountable for disciplined thinking in regard to the state's interests, and it is he who sets the standard for properly advising the policymaker. The thought processes for strategy differ from those of planning and require a different mindset. Theory disciplines strategic thinking by explaining strategy's inherent logic; it serves to remind all involved with policy and strategy neither to promise too much nor fail to consider any of the attributes of strategy. A coherent theory also helps leaders, planners, and others to evaluate, critique, or implement strategy.

3

A Theory Stated: Strategy's Logic

> ... There is an essential unity to all strategic experience in all periods of history because nothing vital to the nature and function of war and strategy changes.[1]
>
> —Colin S. Gray

Strategy provides a coherent blueprint to bridge the gap between the realities of today and a desired future. It is the disciplined calculation of overarching objectives, concepts, and resources within acceptable bounds of risk to create more favorable future outcomes than might otherwise exist if left to chance or in the hands of others. It is the consideration of the relation of how to apply resources to achieve desired results in a specific strategic environment over time. In the context of the state, strategy is the employment of specific instruments of power to achieve the state's political objectives in cooperation or in competition with other actors pursuing their own—possibly conflicting—objectives.[2] Policy, strategy, and planning are all subordinate to the nature of the environment. Strategy has distinct attributes and differs from policy and planning in its scope, assumptions, and premises, but it provides the structure and parameters for more detailed long- and short-term planning. Both strategy and planning use an ends, ways, and means paradigm and are subject to the criteria of suitability, feasibility, and acceptability. Strategy has its own inherent logic that can be understood and applied. Strategy's logic informs strategic thinking for both policy and planning.

An underlying assumption of strategy from a national perspective is that all nation-states and non-state actors have interests that they will pursue to the best of their abilities. Interests are desired end-states categorized in terms such as survival, economic well-being, favorable world order, and promotion of national values. Specific interests are derived from the national values these broad categories summarize as the values play out in the strategic environment. As a result interests can be stated more specifically in the context of circumstances and issues. The elements of power are the raw resources of the state available to promote or advance state interests. Resources are applied through the use of instruments of power derived from these resources.

The role of strategy is to ensure that the pursuit, protection, or advancement of these interests—which is achieved through the application of the instruments of power to specific objectives to create strategic effects in favor of the interest based on policy guidance—is accomplished in a coherent and optimal manner. Strategy is fundamentally about choices; it reflects a preference for a future state or condition and determines how to best get there. In doing so, strategy confronts adversaries, allies, and other actors; and it addresses resource and organizational issues; even then some things will simply remain beyond control or maybe unforeseen.[3] Rational choice, chance and probability, irrational actors, allies, and competitors are all part of the strategic paradigm.[4] Strategy is inherently comprehensive; its foremost purpose is to favorably influence the complex and volatile strategic environment by providing direction for the judicious application of power toward achievement of policy-driven objectives or end-states.[5]

The strategic thought process is all about *how* (concept or way) leadership will use the *power* (resources or means) available to the state to exercise control over sets of circumstances and geographic locations to achieve *objectives* (ends) in accordance with state policy to create strategic effects in support of state interests.[6] Strategy provides direction for the coercive or persuasive use of this power to achieve specified objectives. This direction is by nature proactive, but it is not predictive. Strategy assumes that while the future cannot be predicted, the strategic environment can be studied, assessed, and, to varying degrees, anticipated and manipulated. Only with proper analysis can trends, issues, opportunities, and threats be identified and, with the exception of chance, influenced and shaped through what the state chooses to do or not to do. Thus, good strategy seeks to influence and shape the future environment as opposed to merely reacting to it. Strategy is not crisis management. It is to a large degree its antithesis. Crisis management occurs when there is no strategy or the strategy fails to properly anticipate. Thus, the first premise of a theory of strategy is that strategy is proactive and anticipatory, but not predictive.

A second premise is that political purpose dominates all strategy; this idea has been perhaps best described in Clausewitz' famous dictum, "War is merely the continuation of policy by other means."[7] Political purpose is stated in policy. Policy is the expression of the desired end-state sought by the government. In its finest form, policy is the clear articulation of guidance for the employment of the instruments of power toward the attainment of one or more objectives or end-states. In practice it tends to be much vaguer. Nonetheless, policy dominates strategy by its articulation of the end-state and its guidance regarding resources, limitations on actions, or similar considerations. The analysis of the end-state and guidance in the context of the strategic environment yields strategic objectives. Objectives provide purpose, focus, and justification for the actions embodied in a strategy.[8] Achievement of the objectives creates strategic effects contributing to the desired end-state. National strategy is concerned with a hierarchy of objectives determined by the political purpose. Yet, as Clausewitz notes, that does not mean that policy is a tyrant. The development of strategy informs policy; policy must adapt itself to the realities of the strategic environment and the limits of power. Thus, policy ensures that strategy pursues appropriate aims, while strategy informs policy of the art of the possible.[9]

A third premise is that strategy is contextual and subordinate to the nature of the strategic environment. Strategy is developed from a thorough consideration of the strategic situation and knowledge of the nature of the strategic environment. The strategic environment possesses both physical and metaphysical attributes. Its consideration on any level always has both internal and external components—a duality in its nature that sets up a dialectic leading to multiple orders of effects. On one level the international environment is the external component, consisting of the physical geographic environment, the international system, and other external actors—and their cultures, beliefs, and actions. At this level the domestic environment represents the internal component, consisting of internal physical realities and the internal actors, such as individuals, constituencies, institutions, and organizations, with national security roles within the nation. Indeed, within the United States, there are groups that have significantly different world views than the national leadership, which makes the domestic element of strategy formulation even more complex. Nascent contradictions always exist at every level to challenge the status quo and initiate a search for a new equilibrium. Stability within the environment resists change; instability within the environment entreats a new strategy. The nature of the strategic environment can be described as an interactive, chaotic, complex system of systems. Strategy must be consistent with the context of the strategic situation and the inherent nature of the strategic environment in its formulation and execution.

A fourth premise is that strategy is holistic in outlook. It demands comprehensive consideration. That is to say, while the strategist may be devising a strategy from a particular perspective, he must consider the whole of the strategic environment in his analysis to arrive at a proper strategy to serve

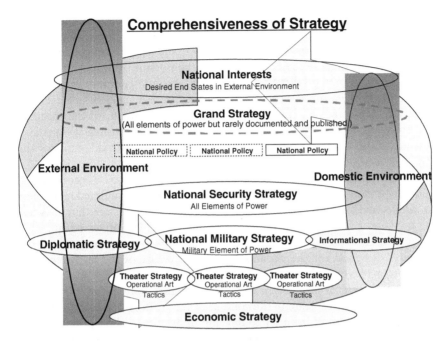

Figure 3.1 Holistic Nature of Strategy.

his intended purpose at his level. He is concerned with external and internal factors at all levels and the horizontal and vertical integration of his strategy. In formulating a strategy, the strategist must also be cognizant that each aspect, objective, concept and resource, has effects on the environment around him. Thus, the strategist must have a comprehensive knowledge of what else is happening within the strategic environment and the potential first-, second-, third-order (and so on) effects of his own choices on the efforts of those above, below, and on his same level, whether they be friendly, adversarial, or indifferent actors. The strategist's efforts must be fully integrated with the strategies or efforts of senior, coordinate, and subordinate elements. Strategists must think holistically—that is comprehensively as depicted in Figure 3.1. They must be cognizant of both the "big picture," their own institution or organization's capabilities and resources and the impact of their actions on the whole of the environment. Good strategy is never developed piecemeal or in isolation. It is systemic thinking at its most complex level.

A fifth premise is that any strategy creates a security dilemma for the strategist and other actors.[10] Strategy may be passive, competitive, or cooperative. However, any strategy, once known or implemented, introduces change into the strategic environment, even when it seeks to maintain the status quo. Change can occur on multiordered levels and may be nonlinear. Change threatens the existing equilibrium or status quo in the strategic environment; raising the question of whether the results of doing nothing are better or worse than the consequences of doing something. Strategy can anticipate the future through the pursuit of proper objectives, but strategy cannot predict the future with absolute certainty, neither the achievement of its objectives nor the precise consequences of achievement or failure. The strategist must determine if the attainment of the specified end-state justifies the risks of initiating action, and the strategist must also consider how other actors may react. Strategy thus poses a dilemma for the strategist and other states and actors.

A sixth premise is that strategy is founded in what is to be accomplished and why it is to be accomplished—strategy cannot be formulated in a policy or intellectual vacuum. The strategist must know the end-state that he is trying to achieve. Strategy rightfully focuses on a desired or preferred end-state among an array of possible end-states in a dynamic environment. Strategy provides direction for the persuasive or coercive use of the instruments of power to achieve specified objectives to create strategic effects leading to the desired end-state. It is essential that the strategist analyze and fully understand the desired end-state in the context of the strategic environment, both internal and external, in order to develop appropriate objectives in regard to the desired end-state. Hence, before proper objectives can be determined, the strategist must comprehend the nature of the strategic environment, the intent of the policy, and the nation's aggregate interests as determinative of necessary and appropriate strategic effects.

A seventh premise is that strategy is an inherently human enterprise. Not solely a consideration of objective factors, " . . . strategy involves human passions, values, and beliefs, few of which are quantifiable."[11] The role of belief systems, world views, and cultural perceptions of all the players is important in the formulation of strategy. Strategists must be careful to eliminate counterproductive bias while ensuring the strategy meets criteria of acceptability at home and abroad—compensating for differences as appropriate.

An eighth premise is that friction is an inherent part of strategy. Friction is the difference between the ideal strategy and the applied strategy—how it is supposed to work versus how it actually unfolds in execution. Friction is a natural consequence of the chaotic and complex nature of the strategic environment, chance, and human frailty.[12] Friction cannot be eliminated, but it can be understood and accounted for by the strategist to a greater or lesser extent in the formulation of the strategy.

A ninth premise is that strategy focuses on root causes and purposes. Such primary foci make strategy inherently adaptable and flexible by emphasizing strategic purpose and empowering subordinate levels. Strategy incorporates learning from experience and is sufficiently broad in its construction to adapt to unfolding events and an adversary's countermoves.[13] Strategy addresses linear and non-linear phenomena. Unlike planning, which is largely cause and effect, strategy is a process interacting with the strategic environment: "strategy is a process, a constant adaptation to shifting conditions and circumstances in a world where chance, uncertainty, and ambiguity dominate."[14] Process is facilitated by constructing strategy with flexibility and adaptability in its component parts. Strategy's focus on root causes and purposes ensures that the direction provided to subordinate levels is sufficiently broad to allow adaptability and flexibility while not deviating from strategic purpose.

A tenth premise is that strategy is hierarchical. The political leadership ensures and maintains its control and influence over the instruments of power through the hierarchical nature of state strategy. Strategy cascades from the national level down to the lower levels. Generally, strategy originates at the top as a consequence of a grand strategy, which may be at work even if undocumented or acknowledged, national security strategy or other stated national-level strategies, and policy statements in regard to specific national powers or issues. Grand and national security strategies lay out broad objectives and directions for the use of all the instruments of power. National policy provides broad strategic guidance from political leaders, generally better articulating the national interests as they relate to specific strategic circumstances. From these strategies and policies the major activities and departments develop subordinate strategies. For the military, a National Defense Strategy and National Military Strategy are derived from the National Security Strategy. In turn, the National Military Strategy leads to theater strategies.

For example, the U.S. Army War College, in consonance with Joint Pub 1-02, defines the levels of strategy as it pertains to the military element of power within the state as:

> *Grand Strategy.* An overarching strategy summarizing the national vision for developing, applying and coordinating all the instruments of national power in order to accomplish the grand strategic objectives of: preserve national security; bolster national economic prosperity; and promote national values. Grand Strategy may be stated or implied.[15]
>
> *National Security Strategy* (also sometimes referred to as Grand Strategy and National Strategy). The art and science of developing, applying and coordinating the instruments of national power (diplomatic, economic, military and informational) to achieve objectives that contribute to national security.[16]
>
> *National Military Strategy.* The art and science of distributing and applying military power to attain national objectives in peace and war.[17]
>
> *Theater Strategy.* The art and science of developing integrated strategic concepts and courses of action directed toward securing the objectives of national and alliance or coalition security policy and strategy by the use of force, threatened use of force, or operations not involving the use of force within a theater.[18]

Figure 3.2 Hierarchical Nature of Strategy.

Other levels of strategy, such as was the case with *The National Defense Strategy of The United States of America*, may be inserted in the hierarchy by leadership at various times.[19] There were nineteen published national-level strategies in addition to the *National Security* Strategy in 2007. The hierarchical nature of strategy facilitates span of control. It provides a logical means of delegating responsibility, authority, and accountability within the senior leadership. It also suggests that if strategy consists of objectives, concepts, and resources, each should be appropriate to the level of strategy and consistent with one another. Thus, strategy at the national military level should articulate military objectives at the national level and express the concepts and resources in terms appropriate to the national level for the specified objective.

At some level, thinking and action fall below the strategic threshold. For example, under the National Military Strategy, the Combatant Commanders develop theater strategy and subsequent campaign plans. At this juncture, the line between strategy and planning blurs with campaign planning that may be either at the theater strategic level or in the realm of pure operational art. Graphically, the relationship between strategy and the levels of war is shown in Figure 3.2.

Within the military structure, strategy differs from operational art and tactics in functional, temporal, and geographic aspects. Functionally and temporally, tactics are the domain of battles, engagements of relative short duration that can be as small as a firefight between two small units or as large as a battle between corps. Operational art is the domain of the campaign, a series of battles taking place over a longer period of time. Strategy is the domain of war that encompasses the spectrum of conflict among nations and other international actors. Tactics is concerned with the parts or pieces, operational art with the combination of the pieces, and strategy with the combinations of these combinations and the desired end-state. Geographically, tactics are very narrowly defined, the operational level is broader and more regional in orientation, and strategy is theater-wide, intercontinental, or global. The time horizon is greater at the strategic level than at the operational and tactical levels. However, it is worth noting that with the advances in transportation and communications there has been a spatial and temporal convergence of strategy, operational art, and tactics. Increasingly, in part due to increasing communications capabilities, individual and isolated events at the tactical level have more immediate and, potentially, greater strategic consequences.[20]

Other departments and agencies that are stewards of the nation's power have similar levels and relationships between strategy and planning. For example, the State Department has strategy at departmental level and planning in support of it. However, it does not have the same familiarity with and adherence to strategy and planning as the Department of Defense. The State Department culture recognizes a direct relationship between individual ambassadors and the president: an ambassador is the president's personal representative to his particular country. Consequently, ambassadors enjoy significant latitude in the exercise of their authority and strategy and planning are more problematic as a result.

An eleventh premise of strategic theory is that strategy has a symbiotic relationship with time. A key component of strategic competency is thinking in time—the ability to foresee continuity of strategic choices with the past and the consequences of their intended and unintended effects in the future. A strategic choice must have continuity with the past as it bridges to the future. Strategy must account for the past in its formulation, acknowledging preceding interaction and history within the strategic environment. A strategic action that has characteristics contrary to the past experience or culture of its own society or the society it affects is less likely to be successful. The strategist extrapolates the possible futures from the present strategic circumstances with a clear sense of the long past from which these possible futures flow; he then constructs a paradigm of change from which planning seeks to shape a more favorable future. Deciding when to undertake a strategy is also critical. If the historical timing is correct, then small actions can have large strategic effects. If the timing is wrong, results invariably take larger efforts and cost more in terms of tangible and intangible resources or produce disappointing results. The strategist is concerned with continuities and change, with both history and the future. History suggests the right questions to ask and provides perspective for the future consequences of the available choices.[21] Futurism identifies the possibilities and probabilities of change. Strategic analysis suggests the actions and timings.

A twelfth premise is that strategy is cumulative. Effects in the strategic environment are cumulative; once enacted, they become a part of the play of continuity and change. Strategy is cumulative from several different perspectives. It is cumulative from the perspective that once implemented, a strategy becomes part of the continuities of the strategic environment. Regardless of whether it is successful or not, it becomes a part of the fabric of change and interaction in the strategic environment, and its consequences must be considered in any future strategy. Strategy is cumulative from a stratified perspective also. The success of a policy is the summation of the strategy and subordinate strategy and planning at all levels and the interaction related to them; the cumulative effect often exceeds the sum of the parts. It is also possible that the value of one level of strategy efforts might be negated by the effects of another level. Strategies at different levels interact and the cumulative effects influence the success of higher and lower strategy and planning over time.

A thirteenth premise is that efficiency is subordinate to effectiveness in strategy. This is not to say that efficiency is not desired. Good strategy is both effective and efficient, but the purpose of strategy is to create strategic effect. Strategic objectives, if accomplished, create or contribute to creation of strategic effects that favor the achievement of the desired end-state at the level of strategy being analyzed and, ultimately, serve national interests. Strategy must emphasize effectiveness because failure, however efficiently executed, creates much greater risk of undesirable and unanticipated multiordered consequences. Concepts and resources serve objectives without undue risk of failure or unintended effects—efficiency is necessarily subordinate to effectiveness in strategy.[22]

A fourteenth premise is that strategy provides a proper relationship or balance among the objectives sought, the methods used to pursue the objectives, and the resources available for the effects sought at its level in the hierarchy. In formulating a strategy, the ends, ways, and means are part of an integral whole and work synergistically to achieve strategic effect at that level of the strategy, as well as contribute to cumulative effects at higher levels. Ends, ways, and means must be in concert qualitatively and quantitatively, both internally and externally. Thus, qualitatively, a National Security Strategy (NSS) objective seeks to achieve the desired effect using any of the necessary and appropriate instruments of power available to the state—the qualitative questions ask whether achieving the objective will produce the strategic effects and whether the effects will justify the objective chosen, the methods used, the resources required, and the social and political costs incurred. A National Military Strategy will identify at the national level appropriate military ends using national military concepts and resources. The National Military Strategy is bounded by the National Security Strategy and is subject to the qualitative questions, but the state cannot logically ask the military to do what it is incapable of accomplishing because of a lack of resources—which is a quantitative relationship. In a similar manner a Theater or Combatant Commander would have appropriate theater-level objectives for which he would develop theater concepts and use resources allocated to his theater in sufficient quantity for his role in the strategy. In some cases concepts might include the integration of other than military instruments of power, if they can be integrated and capabilities and resources are available. In all cases strategy must achieve an acceptably proper balance through consideration of both qualitative and quantitative relationships.

The levels of strategy as well as war are distinct, but interrelated because of the hierarchical and comprehensive nature of strategy and war. Hence, operational or tactical concepts achieve operational or tactical objectives and cannot be elevated to a strategic level even though operational or tactical objectives contribute to the cumulative nature of strategy and actions at these levels on occasion create direct strategic consequences. In a similar manner, strategic objectives and concepts have a proper relationship within a strategy, but must also relate properly within the hierarchy. The quantitative relationship suggests that the concept employs and is resourced with the appropriate types and quantity of resources. From the synergistic balance of ends, ways, and means, the strategy achieves suitability and acceptability—the attainment of the objectives using the instruments of power in the manner envisioned accomplishes the strategic effects desired at acceptable costs. It also achieves feasibility—the strategic concept is executable with the resources made available.

The fifteenth and final premise of strategy is that risk is inherent in all activity. The best the strategist can do is seriously consider the potential risks involved, producing a favorable balance against failure. Strategy is subject to the nature of the strategic environment, and uncertainty is inherent in that environment as a result of chance, nonlinearity, and interaction with other states and actors. Risk can be assessed and often mitigated by reexamining the thinking behind the strategy. For example, what assumptions were made in developing this strategy, and what are the consequences if an assumption is wrong? What internal or external factors are the basis for this strategy? What changes in these factors would enhance or detract from this strategy? What flexibility or adaptability is inherent in the components of the strategy? How can the strategy be modified and at what costs? What are the potential unintended consequences and the costs to recover from them? Nonetheless, no matter how probing the questions, risk of failure will always remain. Failure can be the failure to achieve one's own objectives, providing a significant advantage to one's adversaries, or creating unintended adverse consequences. The risks of failure must be evaluated against the advantages of success and the consequences of not acting.

CONCLUSION

Strategy has an inherent logic that can be understood and applied. It is distinct from planning and serves a unique purpose. It differs from planning in its attributes, scope, assumptions, and premises, but provides the over-all structure and parameters for more detailed long-range and short-term planning. Both strategy and planning use ends, ways, and means, and are bounded by the criteria of suitability, feasibility, and acceptability. Good strategy is founded in a proper understanding and analysis of the strategic environment and national interests and policy, and an understanding of the theory and role of strategy. The strategist accepts that the future cannot be predicted but he believes that it can be anticipated and shaped in favorable terms through creation of judicious strategic effects. Strategic theory guides and disciplines the formulation and implementation of effective strategy.

4

The Strategic Environment

Everything in strategy is very simple, but that does not mean that everything is very easy.[1]

         —Clausewitz

Strategy seeks to cause specific effects in the environment—to advance favorable outcomes and preclude unfavorable outcomes. For the state, the strategic environment is the realm in which the leadership interacts internally and with other states or actors to advance the well-being of the state. This environment consists of the internal and external context, conditions, relationships, trends, issues, threats, opportunities, and interactions, and effects that influence the success of the state in relation to the physical world, other states and actors, chance, and the possible futures. The strategic environment functions as a self-organizing complex system. It seeks to maintain its current relative equilibrium, or to find a new acceptable balance. In this environment some things are known (predictable), some are probable, some are possible, some are plausible, and some remain simply unknown. It is a dynamic environment that reacts to input but not necessarily in a direct cause-and-effect manner. Strategy may focus on a particular interest or policy, but the holistic nature of the environment results in both intended and unintended effects.[2] The strategist ultimately seeks to protect and advance the interests of the state within the strategic environment through creation of multi-ordered effects. Conceptually a model of strategy is simple—ends, ways, and means—but the nature of the strategic environment makes it difficult to apply. To be successful the strategist must comprehend the nature of the strategic environment and construct strategy that is consistent with it, neither denying its nature nor capitulating to other actors or to chance.

The nature of the strategic environment has been described numerous times by different authorities. This environment, encapsulated by the U.S. Army War College in the acronym VUCA, is marked by:

> a world order where the threats are both diffuse and uncertain, where conflict is inherent yet unpredictable, and where our capability to defend and promote our national interests may be restricted by materiel and personnel resource constraints. In short, an environment marked by volatility, uncertainty, complexity, and ambiguity (VUCA).[3]

Characterized by the four earmarks—volatility, uncertainty, complexity, and ambiguity (VUCA)—the strategic environment is always in a greater or less state of dynamic and interdependent instability or "chaos." The role of the strategist is to exercise influence over the volatility, manage the uncertainty, simplify the complexity, and resolve the ambiguity, all in terms favorable to the interests of the state and in compliance with policy guidance.

The VUCA thinking argues that the strategic environment is volatile. It is subject to rapid and explosive reaction and change, often characterized by violence. Uncertainty also characterizes this environment, which is inherently problematic and unstable. New issues appear, and old problems repeat or reveal themselves in new ways so that past solutions are dubious, and the perceived greater truth often vacillates with time. Everything is subject to question and change. This environment is extremely complex. It is composed of many parts that are intricately related in such a manner that understanding them collectively or separating them distinctly is extremely difficult and often impossible. Sometimes the environment is so complicated or entangled that complete understanding and permanent solutions are improbable. The strategic environment is also characterized by ambiguity. The environment can be interpreted from multiple perspectives with various conclusions that may suggest a variety of equally attractive solutions, some of which will prove to be good and others bad. Certain knowledge is often lacking and intentions may be surmised, but never entirely known. The VUCA thinking describes the appearance of the environment without providing a theoretical understanding of it. Since the role of the strategist is ultimately to advocate actions that will lead to desirable outcomes while avoiding undesirable ones, the strategist must understand the nature of the environment in order to exert influence within it.[4]

The nature of the strategic environment, as the VUCA acronym suggests, is difficult to grasp and is perhaps the most challenging task of strategic thinking. Yet, understanding its nature explains policy and strategy's possibilities and limitations, and provides the insight and parameters for articulating strategic objectives, concepts, and resources. Two theories—chaos theory and complexity theory—serve as appropriate metaphors for understanding the nature of the strategic environment and providing an analogous description of its attributes and functioning. While founded in abstract mathematical extrapolations, these two theories capture the essence of the observed VUCA behavior of the strategic environment and have been adapted by some political scientists to describe the international strategic environment. Some even suggest these theories might be applied directly to the evaluation and selection of strategic choices, but that is not the purpose of their use in this book.[5] Here, chaos theory and complexity theory are used to help the strategist to think conceptually and pragmatically about the nature of the functioning of the strategic environment.

Chaos theory was popularized by Edward Lorenz, a diligent meteorologist who, while searching for a way to produce more accurate weather predictions, discovered the "butterfly effect." He noticed that miniscule changes in his initial input to mathematical calculations for weather predictions could have extraordinary and unpredictable effects on the outcomes. He concluded that the future behavior of complex and dynamic systems is incredibly sensitive to tiny variations in initial conditions.[6] Over 150 years earlier, Clausewitz understood and described this phenomenon in war and wrapped it into his definition of friction: "Everything in war is very simple, but the simplest thing is difficult. The difficulties accumulate and end by producing a kind of friction that is inconceivable unless one has experienced war."[7] Likewise, folklore captured this same reality: "For want of a nail, the shoe was lost; for want of a shoe, the horse was lost; for want of a horse..., the kingdom was lost!" Computers allowed scientists to do the calculations to study this effect in mathematically simple systems, thereby illuminating the "chaotic" behavior of the strategic environment and other complex systems.

Chaos theory is a different way of viewing reality. Prior to the development of chaos theory, two world views dominated thinking. Systems were defined as deterministic and predictable, or random and disordered—thus unpredictable. Deterministic systems are predictable because the same inputs will yield the same outputs every time the experiment is conducted. In math's chaos theory, chaos is not a state of utter confusion—random, unpredictable, and uncontrollable—but an observable reality that adheres to certain rules even as it appears chaotic in the evident sense. It explains observed physical behavior that possesses characteristics in common with both order *and* randomness as opposed to the more traditional either orderliness *or* randomness. Put more scientifically, chaos theory describes unstable aperiodic behavior in deterministic nonlinear dynamical systems. A dynamical system is one that interacts and changes over time. Behavior in chaotic systems is aperiodic, meaning that no variable describing the state of the system undergoes a regular repetition of values—each changes in some part over time. The behavior in a chaotic system continues to manifest the effects of any small difference, and consequently a *precise* prediction of a future state in a given system that is aperiodic is not possible. On the other hand, chaotic behavior as a mathematical phenomenon does possess structure or patterns and, as a consequence, can be predicted and influenced to some extent, with the most influence occurring in the initial conditions.[8]

Chaos theory is important because it helps explain why deterministic or linear systems sometimes produce unpredictable behavior. Chaos theory also demonstrates that much that appears as random, in reality is not—there are indirect cause-and-effect relationships at work, sometimes not detectable. The deterministic nature of a chaotic system ensures there is some manifestation of continuity from one state to the next, while the nonlinearity means that the consequences of any changes may appear as spontaneous and extreme. In a chaotic system, early changes can have an extraordinary effect on the long term, but the results are bounded from the extremity of total randomness. Thus, chaotic systems are a mixture of continuities and change. The strategic environment can be viewed as a chaotic system in which human history represents aperiodic behavior—broad patterns in the rise and fall of civilizations are evident, but no event is ever repeated exactly.[9]

Complexity theory also offers insights into the nature of the strategic environment, often shared by or augmenting chaos theory. The strategic environment is by definition a complex system. A system exists when a set of elements are interconnected so that changes in some elements or their relations produce changes in other parts of the system, and the system taken as a whole exhibits properties and behaviors that are different from those of the sum of the parts. Systems are generally dynamic, and social, or humanistic, systems are especially so. Systems may be very large or very small, and in some complex systems, large and small components live cooperatively. Complexity occurs in both natural and man-made systems. The level of complexity depends on the character of the systems, the environment, and the nature of the interactions among them. The different parts of complex systems are linked and affect one another in a synergistic manner through both positive and negative feedback. In a complex system, the numerous independent elements continuously interact and spontaneously self-organize and adapt for survival in increasingly more elaborate and sophisticated structures over time. Cause and effect are not proportional to each other and often cannot be related. Such a system is neither completely deterministic nor completely random, but rather exhibits both characteristics—adhering to the chaos theory model. Complex systems, therefore, are not precisely predictable, and the sum of their interactions is greater than the parts.

Complex systems appear to naturally evolve to a state of self-organized criticality, at which time they lay on the border of order and disorder, teetering on the "edge of chaos." At the point where a complex, dynamical, chaotic system becomes sufficiently unstable, an attractor (such as a minor event similar to Lorenz's insignificant mathematical changes) instigates the stress, and the system splits. This is called bifurcation—the point at which significant change occurs, and the newly resulting systems are distinct from the original while still having continuities. The edge of chaos is important; it is the stage when the system can carry out the most complex computations and the point when both opportunities (positive feedbacks) and threats (negative feedbacks) are greatest. If the system cannot maintain its balance, it seeks a new equilibrium. At the point of bifurcation, little changes produce great outcomes.[10]

Chaos and complexity theories offer a perspective that describes the strategic environment as it is, as opposed to a direct and simplistic cause-and-effect linear model. These theories recognize that the world is composed of both linear and nonlinear dynamics. Grasping this distinction is critical to the kind of analysis the policymaker and strategist undertakes! Complexity theory does not seek prediction but understanding of the various elements of the environment and the actors involved. It offers a complex world view that accepts contradictions, anomalies, and dialectic processes. It alerts the strategist to the existence of multicausal situations, unintended consequences, circumstances ripe for change, the roles of feedback and self-fulfilling expectations, and other abnormalities discounted, or even disparaged, by the rational planning model.[11]

Chaos and complexity theories serve as useful metaphors for the strategic environment because they provide insights to VUCA phenomena and the relationship between the strategic environment and strategy. The strategic environment is composed of elements representing both continuity and change. Relationships and interaction are the keys to understanding the nature and dynamism of the strategic environment. Characterized by instability and aperiodic behavior, it does not repeat itself precisely, although situations may closely approximate those of the past. Thus, it possesses the attributes of both linearity and nonlinearity. The strategic environment is deterministic in that change is bounded by a variety of factors, including, to some degree, by what has occurred before. It will have continuities, but the exact nature and extremity of change are not necessarily predictable because of its non-linear attributes. The strategic environment is often particularly sensitive to early changes at critical times, and the outcomes are often not proportional to the inputs, thus creating unpredictable and at times unintended outcomes.

Major changes at the strategic level often can have very simple causes. Any change that occurs creates feedback (effect), which eventually must be accounted for within the equilibrium of the strategic environment. Chaotic behavior is more evident in long-term systems than in short-term systems. This observation illuminates why planning's shorter time horizons supports more certainty than strategy's longer view. At the same time, a chaotic system actually can evolve in a way that appears to be smooth and ordered, suggesting that strategy is practical and can produce favorable results.

Strategy therefore must account for the chaotic, complex nature of the strategic environment, and shape it by creating and anticipating effects in order to be successful.[12]

Often referred to as a *system of systems* in order to emphasize its complexity, the strategic environment is a composite of complex systems, linked vertically and horizontally. As such, the strategic environment exhibits complex, self-organizing behavior—it continuously seeks to find an acceptable order or relative balance in which it can exist. Its complexity results from individual decisions or acts and the interactions resulting from the decisions or changing circumstances. Its numerous parts and agents act individually or collectively, according to their own circumstances and interests. In acting, these parts and agents can globally affect the circumstances and interests of all other parts or agents. Some of the interactions are predicable, some are chaotic, and some are stochastic (determined by chance). What this means is that the strategic environment is inherently uncertain, and that unpredictability must be taken as a natural part of the system. As a result, traditional ideas of control—direct cause and effect—are not as applicable. We find instead a form of control that is macroscopic, not seeking to impose precise domination over details because these are inherently uncontrollable at the strategic level. Strategy provides broad, meaningful direction and structure suitable to the changing complexity of the strategic environment—retaining adaptability and flexibility by directing actions to favorably alter the environment rather than trying to control it absolutely.[13]

As the theories illustrate, all complex systems are inherently nonlinear, and outcomes cannot be predicted or understood by the simple act of adding up the parts and the relationships. In linear systems, changes in output are nearly proportional to input; the sum of the inputs equals the output in a more-or-less predictable fashion. Most people think from a linear perspective and in a linear fashion, and indeed planning operates in large measure on linear assumptions even though practical experience often belies this approach. The difference is accounted for in planning with reserve forces and planned branches and sequels. In a system at the strategic level, complexity enters the simplest actions, no matter how deterministic they appear. The effect of one action may depend on or conflict with the status of another variable, and the net effect may change the conditions that affect other or all variables. On a primary level, then, to understand outcomes the strategist must examine his own choices in light of the goals, resources, and policies of all other actors and the continuities and variables of the rest of the strategic environment. Strategic acts are not one-sided, and the opposing or other actors may make choices in regard to responding to an action or even preempt it, so that the complexity confronting the strategist is compounded by what the other actors may choose to do. On yet another level, the chaotic nature of complex systems means that initial behaviors and outcomes cause changes that produce unintended dynamics with cascading effects that can alter, limit, enhance, or otherwise affect future choices or require reaction.[14] Thus the nonlinear characteristics of the strategic environment result from the interaction among chance and subordinate or integral self-organizing and adaptive systems—states, other actors, and the physical world.

Nonlinearity suggests a world in which the future has both continuities and unpredicted threats and opportunities. It suggests an interactive process in which strategic choices produce effects that in turn generate reactions that may or may not create major or complex changes. Other actors— friendly, adversarial, or indifferent—with regard to a strategy's objectives may choose to act, react, or preempt. The smallest "friction," whether by lack of foresight, slow execution, or factors beyond the actor's control, can amplify itself into a cascade of things going wrong to create potential chaos. Further, chance events, purely stochastic phenomena, occur and shape the strategic environment in favor of or against the strategy. And, of course, actors, friction, and chance function interactively to further influence the strategic environment and affect the strategy.

Thus, the world is more a place of instability, discontinuity, synergies, and unpredictability than planners prefer. Although a meaningful degree of linearity can be achieved, results often vary from the original intent, at times costing more than anticipated because of the need to manage the chaos within the strategic environment over the strategy's timeline. Thus, in the strategy process, scientific analysis must be combined with historical perspective to create a comprehensive strategy that provides for dynamic change, innovation, responsiveness, flexibility, and adaptability.[15] The *art of strategy* allows the strategist to see the nature of the strategic environment and a path or multiple paths to his desired end-states; and the *scientific aspect of strategy* provides a disciplined methodology to describe the path in a rational expression of ends, ways, and means that shape the strategic environment in favorable terms.

As a complex system, the strategic environment is interactive and adaptive because the states and actors have the capacity to respond individually and collectively (in a myriad of bilateral and multilateral relationships) to new challenges to the relationships and structures that provided stability in the past. When the balance is lost, the states and actors, individually and collectively, seek to self-organize their patterns of behavior into new patterns intended either to restore the former equilibrium or to obtain changes favorable to their interests. As in any complex system, to do this they must accommodate change, changing or responding in ways that provide for success in the new environment. At the same time, continuities with the past remain and are embedded in the emergent order. The adaptive task for the state or other actor is to maintain an acceptable balance between internal needs and external demands; sufficient actions and resources must be dedicated to the demands of the external environment, but at the same time the needs and expectations of the domestic environment must be appropriately

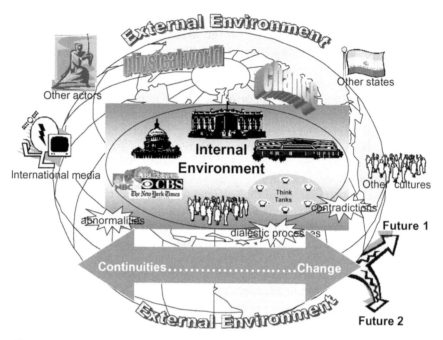

Figure 4.1 Strategic Environment: A System of Systems.

addressed. The actors must adapt more or less in concert with the strategic environment; making external adjustments with their relationships with each other and the overall environment in order to survive.

If sufficient coevolution does not occur—whether because of a lack of adaptability on the part of leadership, insufficient material resources, or whatever other reason—one or more states or actors and their internal systems collapse, and new structures and relationships emerge in their place. This process of adaptation and change does not have to occur continuously or evenly; varying periods of stasis may be punctuated by rapid change until a new equilibrium is reached. Given this phenomenon, small events can some times seemingly trigger major changes—the so-called "butterfly effect." In a similar manner, small decisions made or not made early in a period of environmental change can have a dramatic impact, possibly leading to irreversible consequences that may result in significantly different outcomes than would otherwise be the case. The strategist can fall victim to this phenomena—reacting to its consequences—or, through judicious study and assessment, seek to use it to advance the interests of the state.

Again, the strategic environment is a complex system consisting of systems within systems as depicted in Figure 4.1. The strategist must recognize that, to be successful, a strategy must account for the internal and external components of the various systems composing the strategic environment and the multiordered effects caused by the relationships within and among them. For the political state, these components can be summarized as the domestic and international environments on a grand scale, but external elements can be further divided into adversaries, allies, and other actors. In addition, the physical or natural environment is both an internal and external element, acting as another complex system within the strategic environment. The domestic environment can be subdivided into the general public, interest groups, other parts of the governmental bureaucracy, and the sub-systems or actors of the strategist's own organization. The strategic environment on all its levels is characterized by VUCA, but to say that the strategic environment is VUCA is not to say that it defies study, analysis, and evaluation, or that future changes or developments cannot be anticipated. It is simply to say that to predict or control it with any significant degree of certainty is exceptionally complex and difficult. The chaotic and complex nature of the strategic environment has implications for the development of strategy at all levels.

Like any complex system, the international environment is constantly subjected to change, experiencing periods of stability and instability. Instability tends to increase as the level of interaction rises, particularly if one or more actors seek to impose change on the strategic environment. Periods exhibiting lower levels of interaction are generally more stable. Periods characterized by stability tend to favor problem-solving linear approaches to issues or challenges, while periods exhibiting greater instability tend to require nonlinear perspectives and problem-defining approaches. As the level or complexity of interaction rises, the strategic environment potentially moves into a state of self-organizing criticality, at which time it lies on the border of order and disorder, and then is highly susceptible to a radical new rebalancing. The strategic equilibrium is adjusted continuously, but on these occasions the strategic environment experiences dramatic change. Such major changes really reflect upheavals in the key continuities of the strategic environment. Strategists in the first quarter of the twenty-first century must recognize that the emerging strategic environment is the product of such an upheaval. In terms of chaos or complexity theory, the strategic environment is in the process of bifurcation. The order or relative balance of the bipolar Cold War becomes part of the past as a new order is formed. While not all the rules must change, many will need to be changed or reinterpreted as states and actors seek a new equilibrium.

What is the nature of this new strategic environment? A vast array of existing literature that attempts to grasp or describe the new strategic environment in terms meaningful to different communities—business, government, academic, military, and religion—is available.[16] What they share in common is an appreciation that the strategic environment is in the midst of a major reshaping as a result of changes generally attributed to the convergence of a number of events or trends: the end of the Cold War; massive changes in economic relationships; the rise of globalization; and seminal advances in technology. At the heart of these changes is the "establishment of information and knowledge—their production, dissemination, storage, and use—as the fundamental social and economic activity, rather than the cultivation of agriculture or the production of manufactured goods."[17] It is a transformation of social and economic life on a global scale. Such a widespread change in multiple subsystems has dramatic implications for the strategic environment and the states and actors that comprise the international system. Moreover, it will impose further change both at the international and domestic levels of most, if not all, actors.

This period of great and rapid change presents both threats and opportunities. The period has already revealed its characteristics in broad terms. It favors service economies over industrial manufacturing economies; it is global and local in scope at the same time—global in its reach and local in its focus; it allows and encourages decentralized production while it democratizes decision making; it challenges and replaces authorities who cannot compete; and it appears to be ushering in a period of hypercompetition among businesses, cultures, and nation-states or other new state-like actors.[18] In essence, it will be a period of revolutionary change until a new equilibrium is achieved, with the strategic environment now teetering on the edge of chaos. It is a period of great opportunity and risk for the strategist in any system. In retrospect, the latter Cold War period appears to have been relatively stable, with its established rules for the international strategic environment that orchestrated the relationships and interaction among the states and actors—in short, an acceptable equilibrium.

CONCLUSION

Strategy is made difficult by the chaotic and complex nature of the strategic environment. It represents a daunting challenge for the national security professional in whatever role, but it is this very nature that justifies a policy debate and a discipline of strategy—otherwise, planning would suffice. If chaos and complexity theories apply, the radical alteration of the strategic environment that resulted from the end of the Cold War offers even greater opportunities and challenges as the strategic environment reorders itself toward a new and as-yet undefined equilibrium in the twenty-first century. The roles of the strategist and national security professional are even more critical in this period as policymakers seek help in ensuring that the reshaping of the strategic environment occurs in terms favorable to the state. The professional's role increases in importance as the instability and difficulty increase. Yet, the fundamental tasks remain the same: understand the nature of the strategic environment and its various subsystems and construct policy and strategy that focus the state on its long-term well-being. How well the policymaker and strategist are able to do this depends on their ability to anticipate the interaction within the strategic environment and to develop appropriate strategic actions to serve national interests.

5

Theory in the Real World

In theory there is no difference between theory and practice. In practice there is.

—Yogi Berra

If strategy is simply the calculation of objectives, concepts, and resources within acceptable bounds of risk to create more favorable possibilities than might otherwise exist by chance or at the hands of others, why do effective strategies so often appear to elude the strategist? The answer, of course, is that successful strategy is much more complex than the calculation of objectives, concepts, and resources. Strategic theory in the real world confronts the dynamic nature of the strategic environment and the mind of the strategist—how strategists approach strategy-making in the context of their strategic environments. It also depends on the caliber of the execution of the strategy. Good strategy flows from understanding the nature of the environment and *creating a symmetry and synergy of objectives, concepts, and resources* that offer the best probability of achieving the policy aims. The strategist is assisted by the logic of strategy and the construct of planning, but the strategist is not a planner. Good strategy formulation provides for flexibility and adaptability so that planning and execution can be tailored to more immediate circumstances and respond to unanticipated opportunities and constraints. Good strategy remains, however, valid in its focus and direction and achieves its intent even when these opportunities and constraints are taken into account. This chapter discusses the implications of the environment for strategy development, the necessary and distinct mind-set required of the strategist, and the kinds of obstacles encountered as the theory of strategy is practised in the real world. It precedes and sets up chapters dealing with the international and domestic environments, the strategic appraisal, and the strategy formulation process. While focused on strategy, it offers insights for all national security professionals involved in the formulation and implementation of policy and strategy.

IMPLICATIONS OF THE STRATEGIC ENVIRONMENT

Strategists must comprehend the nature of the environment in which the strategy they are formulating is to be applied—understand the kind of world they live in or the one that will emerge.[1] As advanced in Chapter 4 with the analogies of chaos and complexity theories, the strategic environment is not totally random, unpredictable, or uncontrollable. Rather, the environment exhibits some characteristics of both randomness and order. Change may be induced in it by design or chance, but, because of its complexity, any change may produce results totally out of proportion to the initiating change—either greater or lesser than anticipated—and thus a degree of uncertainty and unpredictability is inherent to its nature. Changes come from actors, interactive circumstances, or chance. Actors may introduce rational and irrational changes through action or selective inaction, or through simple indifference or ignorance. Yet, many strategists reduce strategy to overly linear and detailed directives that do not allow for the flexibility and adaptability to accommodate such unpredictability.

On the other hand, much of the strategic environment is deterministic and adheres to certain rules; continuities guide its general behavior over time, and extend—to varying degrees—into periods of major upheaval and new equilibriums. These rules are both physical, as is the case with gravity, geography, and weather, and incorporeal. Rules of international behavior are an example of an incorporeal continuity. When in effect, these rules bound what is workable and acceptable within the international environment. Continuities may be codified and thus formally acknowledged, or may just be accepted practices. In some cases, they exist below the awareness level of the actors in the environment. Continuities always seek to reassert themselves, but their validity cannot be taken for granted. Continuities can be leveraged so that a strategy is assisted by the environment's natural inclinations, thus moving with the flow of history. Collective security is arguably a continuity that emerged in the twentieth century and may be leveraged into the twenty-first century. On the other hand, a particular continuity's role may not be the same even though it still exists. Gravity continued to exist after the invention of the airplane, but its affect on warfare changed. Too few strategists critically consider the role of continuities in strategy development, missing opportunities, or making invalid assumptions. For example, with the collapse of the Soviet Union, many strategists focused on the promises of liberal capitalism and globalization and missed the implications of the resurgence of the continuities of nationalism and religion. Critical examination of continuities and change focuses the strategist on what needs to change, what continuities can be leveraged for the necessary changes, and what should not or cannot be changed. All are important!

Understanding the strategic environment as a system of systems is a daunting intellectual challenge. Each system within it has internal and external components—and all interrelate to varying degrees. The multilayered interaction results in complexity and nonlinearity. The chaotic nature of this interaction is difficult to fathom, and it is even more difficult to manipulate effectively. Nothing is ever quite what it seems and all is subject to greater or lesser changes. It is a world of unlimited possibilities and seemingly great promise, tempered by competing interests and often unclear or less than desirable alternatives. Much appears insidious and Machiavellian or subject to nature and chance. Policy is often stated in lofty and idealistic terms with too little regard for political reality and available resources—leaving the strategist without practical goals and adequate resources. All are interrelated, often confusing and convoluted, and very complex. A strategist or national security professional must be comfortable in the VUCA (volatility, uncertainty, complexity, and ambiguity) environment. Too few of either are prepared for this actuality.

The strategist is immersed in the complexity of the system of systems represented by the strategic environment. For example, a U.S. strategist assigned to NATO (North Atlantic Treaty Organization) sees it from a national perspective as an external component even as he works within NATO to shape the rest of the international environment. Within NATO, he is an internal part of an organizational actor in the international environment. The complexity of relationships and interactions grows exponentially. The domestic environment is an internal component of the strategic environment relative to any national defense strategy. It consists of domestic actors, constituencies, institutions, and organizational roles as well as the physical realities of resources and capabilities. The military strategist is confronted with the domestic interaction of individuals, media, special interest groups, civilian think tanks, branches of government, other departments of the executive branch, and offices and sub-organizations within DOD (Department of Defense} itself. Thus, any strategy is subject to interaction and reaction with domestic interests and actors, the nuances of interests within the strategist's own organization, and the interests and actors of the international arena. Some domestic actors may actually be working at odds with the strategist, trying to frustrate his efforts for political or other reasons. Too few national security professionals are willing or capable of accepting and working with this complexity and nonlinearity. Strategy remains in the too-hard box, and insufficient time and resources are devoted to its consideration. As a result, strategic thinking is often reduced to simple assumptions that are often ill-founded, but misleadingly seem to allow "strategy" to unfold like good planning. Strategists must study and assess the whole environment and then shape it by the design and articulation of strategy.

Strategy is too critical to be ignored or placed at risk by virtue of erroneous assumptions or by relegating it to a planning model. Strategic environments may be difficult to assess, but good strategy—which must be based on sound strategic-level thinking—can shape the environment more positively than chance or lack of strategic direction. For as surely as uncertainty characterizes the future; the future will nonetheless come: "Strategy abhors a vacuum: if the strategic function is lacking, strategic effect will be generated by the casual accumulation of tactical and operational outcomes."[2] Carefully crafted strategic initiatives bound future results into outcomes more acceptable to policymakers than those offered by chance, expediency, or adversaries. As chaos theory suggests, early actions can have a disproportionate affect on the overall pattern of change in the strategic environment. Strategists, particularly when over-focused on immediate demands of decision makers, often fail to look to the future with sufficient depth of analysis and act too late to create positive strategic effects at relatively low costs. Relying on expediency and planning methodologies in lieu of proper strategic thinking ignores the advantages that accrue from intended cumulative effects and increases the costs for and risks to the state's security.

The strategic environment can be analyzed from different perspectives. In this text the reader is asked to consider it from the perspective of systems within systems *interacting* in both linear and nonlinear ways. The strategist must understand the systems, but the proper focus of strategy is on the dimensions of interaction. Strategy has many dimensions, and all are in play to a greater or lesser extent at all times. A weakness in considering any one dimension can prove fatal to the whole enterprise. Colin S. Gray suggests that there are seventeen or more of these dimensions: people, society, culture, politics, ethics, economics and logistics, organization, administration, information and intelligence, strategic theory and doctrine, technology, operations, command, geography, friction/chance/uncertainty, adversary, and time. These must be considered holistically—that is, individually— but at the same time in context with the others.[3] Some have argued that the transformation of strategy has occurred over the last 2, 400 years on a larger and more integrated scale. They would list the major dimensions as bureaucracy, mass politics, ideology, technology, and economic power. Here, too, it is recognized that the interaction among these affect outcomes exponentially.[4] History makes clear that particular dimensions play a greater role or are more critical at particular times, and that none can be ignored over time. Hence, as the Cold War wound down and the new world order began to emerge, ideology (communism versus liberal capitalism) appeared to wane in importance only to reemerge in the Global War On Terrorism (radical Islam versus secularism). It matters significantly what the topic of confrontation or the dimension of competition or collaboration is in developing a strategy. An economic issue may demand a conceptualization or model of interaction different from an ideological one and a different weighting of effort among the instruments of power. Just so, any other dimension may be affected, and all must be considered in the development of a strategy. As a complex system of systems, the strategic environment may evolve into new dimensions that must also be considered. Many strategists think too little about interaction, the dimensions in which it occurs and the relationships among the dimensions.

All strategy is about "the future." The future is where strategy has its effect. In dealing with unknowns and uncertainties, strategy forecasts from a knowledge and understanding of the systems of the strategic environment—what they are (facts and assumptions) and how they interact (observation, reason, and assumptions) within the dimensions of strategy. From this understanding the strategist derives the key factors that contribute causally to the achievement of policy aims—assisting or precluding success. These factors may be tangible or intangible, representing any aspect of the environment. The existence of other states and actors, internal and external, is one of many factors that must be considered in any strategy development effort. Key strategic factors constitute the key facts, continuities, and emerging trends—they are at the point of interaction within the system and among systems. In strategy formulation these factors are keys to developing an effective strategy because using or influencing them is how policy goals are achieved and interests realized. The strategist seeks to change, leverage, or overcome these, in effect modifying the equilibrium within the strategic environment to support policy aims. Balancing continuities and emerging trends is the most intellectually challenging task in developing strategy—seeking to address one aspect of a complex system without inducing unfavorable ripple effects elsewhere in the system. The strategist's assessment of how to best do this is reflected in his selection of ends, ways, and means—the rational output of strategic thought. Too often in strategy development, insufficient analysis is applied to the identification and use of key factors, and as a consequence decisive strategic factors are often overlooked, misidentified, or ill addressed.

Strategy is about thinking big and over time. Strategic thinking is not about reductionism, although the strategy will eventually be simplified and stated clearly as ends, ways, and means. Strategic thinking is about thoroughness and holistic thinking. It seeks to understand and affect the whole positively by a comprehensive appreciation of the synergistic interdependence of the parts and the interactions among them—the effects they have on one another in the past, present, and anticipated future. It shares this perspective with chaos and complexity theories. Articulating strategic thinking as ends, ways, and means is only one step in a sophisticated intellectual process seeking to create a synthesis of consensus, efforts, and circumstances to influence the overall environment favorably while managing the risks involved in pursuing opportunities or reacting to threats.[5] While ends, ways, and means get at the essence of the strategy and must flow from strategic perspective, thus collectively creating the strategic effect, they do not obviate an explanation of "why," one of the paramount purposes of strategy. A strategy must work on different planes and speak to different audiences. In this sense, another purpose of strategy formulation is to explain and forecast in order to generate a domestic and foreign consensus in favor of the policy pursued. To do this, strategy must have a sense of where the state has been and where it is headed. Anything less in regard to the past "is to neglect the direction in which the historical winds have been blowing. And the best grand strategies, like the most efficient navigators, keep the winds behind them."[6] Anything less in regard to the future is to strike blindly into the dark at nothing, even while asking others to follow you into the darkness. Balancing continuities of the past and emerging possibilities is essential; a strategy must articulate the transition from the past state to the future in a manner that resonates with multiple audiences.

As a result of the complexity of the environment, strategy inherently creates a "security dilemma" for other states and actors that must be considered. Actions taken or not taken by one state or actor always have the potential to affect other states and actors, particularly their role in the strategic environment and their perception of that role. Any action risks changing the status quo for friends and adversaries alike, creating an element of instability in the equilibrium, and introducing an element of risk for all. Because of its chaotic nature, the environment is subject to unintended multiordered effects and chance.[7] Strategy is never to be undertaken lightly and must be approached comprehensively. At the state level, according to MacGregor Knox, "violence, chance, and politics; danger and friction; escalatory interaction between adversaries remain the terrain of those who make strategy."[8] The stakes are always potentially high! Many strategists too often focus on one-dimensional first-order effects, foregoing consideration of multiordered effects, how a strategy will be perceived by others, or the role of chance. In failing to properly consider the multidimensional and multiordered effects, strategists increase the potential risks.

Effects in the strategic environment are cumulative, but can be accommodated or nullified by interactions within the system, counterstrategies, or chance. As a complex system of systems, the environment seeks an equilibrium that allows its subsystems to coexist. As subsystems, states and other actors seek to survive or advance in the environment according to what they deem acceptable and the system will tolerate. Changes can cancel one another in whole or part—although states and actors tend to have long memories, and important interests persevere. Once a change becomes part of the fabric of the environment, it lingers, influencing the nature of future change. It then becomes one level of consideration among many for future strategies but often reemerges in a different context. Much of this activity may appear below the noise level of the strategist, but the role of the strategist is to be aware of what and who influence the well-being of the state and how. Too few strategists give consideration to the role of continuities—what they are, the roles they play and when they are important to strategy.

As a chaotic, complex system, the strategic environment is also time sensitive—timing and rate of change matters. Somewhat paradoxically, periods of stability are the best time to contemplate bold shifts in strategy and the most difficult time to get a decision to do it. The environment is always rebalancing itself at the margins, and states apply the nuances of diplomacy and force in a peaceful world very carefully. At such times of relative stability, strategy rightfully focuses on what the state wants to achieve and then considers how the state will accomplish its goals over the long term. Yet few decision makers are willing to risk disturbances in the equilibrium or expend political capital for future gains without a clear threat or clarion opportunity, particularly in a democratic state. This makes it difficult to advocate strategies to preclude major upheavals in the environment. Thus, the governments of France and Great Britain appeased Germany during the 1930s instead of confronting it. President Franklin D. Roosevelt was able to move the United States only incrementally, and relatively insufficiently, toward preparedness for World War II. Yet, strategy serves the state best when it anticipates and leads change. Preemptive or proactive strategies—or well-articulated grand strategies—too often are ignored by the strategic community as a result of the preference for near-term stability and the avoidance of political risk.

When the strategic equilibrium is disrupted in a major way, in chaos theory termed as potential bifurcation, the more numerous, rapid, and complex changes require a much more responsive strategy. Again, paradoxically, periods of major instability are the best time to advocate bold, broad strategies but provide the least time for consideration, thus magnifying the risk. Here decision makers perceive the risks of not changing to be greater than the risks of adopting a bold strategy. Thus, Japan's attack on Pearl Harbor opened the way for Roosevelt to go to war to defeat Japan and the Axis Powers. But the Roosevelt administration, in concert with its allies, used success in the war to establish a "new world order" defined by the establishment of the United Nations and the institutions for international finance. In periods of great instability, strategy making is accelerated but can be enhanced by the strategist's preparation prior to the upheaval. The strategist who fully comprehends the nature of the environment and its continuities and manifestations during periods of stability can leverage this mastery during such periods. This leverage could be particularly useful if the instability cannot be preempted favorably through proactive strategies. Such mastery also allows the clarification of what constitutes well-being and anticipates objectives, while fostering familiarity with potential courses of action and resource requirements. In the unstable environment, the strategist gives great consideration to the multiordered effects of the rate and significance of change, and the fact that predictability decreases as change increases in rate and scope. This means that change itself is magnified in the process and must be managed carefully. In these circumstances, the strategist must compete on the edge, creating a relentless flow of competitive advantages that collectively move the state forward in the preferred strategic direction. The demands upon the strategist and strategy differ from those of a stable environment in that they are now confronting less clear boundaries, less predictable adversaries and allies, a more VUCA-like future, less time in which to develop strategy, or various combinations of these factors. In such an environment, the strategist anticipates whenever possible, reacts when necessary, and leads when circumstances are right.[9] Strategists must prepare themselves in times of stability for periods of instability by mastering knowledge and understanding of the many subsystems and their interdependence, as well as the whole of the strategic environment.

The strategic environment readily compares to a chaotic, complex system. To be successful the strategist and national security professional must understand its nature and implications for the development of good strategies that advance and protect the interests of the state. It requires that the professional maintains a level of interest and knowledge in the past, the present, and the future and immerse himself in the continued study of the strategic environment.

THE STRATEGIST'S MIND-SET

Strategic thinking is both an art and science and an essential element for success in the national security community. True strategic genius is able to comprehend the nature of the strategic environment, especially its complexity and multiordered interactions, and derive rational ends, ways, and means that solicit consensus and create strategic effects leading to the desired end-state. Not all senior officials can aspire to reach the apex of strategic skill, but all senior leaders should be able to evaluate and execute a coherent and relevant strategy. In this regard, a proper understanding of the strategist's mind-set further helps the national security professional, genius or not, to assess his role and responsibilities in regard to strategy. Leadership can delegate the strategy formulation function to strategic genius if it is present and can be recognized, but the leader retains responsibility for the quality of both the strategy and its implementation.

Strategy is essentially a human enterprise, with all of humanity's genius, frailties, and shortcomings. It is both an individual and collective undertaking that bears fruit from its successful anticipation of requirements and effects and the successful execution of its methodology. The strategist and the implementers of strategy are actors pitted against other actors—including other strategists, circumstance, and chance in the chaotic and complex strategic environment. History is replete with examples of people making irrational, as opposed to rational decisions, and wrong rational decisions based on inaccurate information and assumptions. Study can help gain insight into human behavior, but simplicity, stability, and universality do not apply to human behavior, even as assumptions about human behavior help us deal with it.[10] As a human enterprise every aspect of strategy is subject to exception, and the strategist must be open to this reality. This reality extends to all actors, whether they are participants, allies, enemies, potential adversaries, or seemingly disinterested onlookers.

Ideology and culture are powerful influences on the shaping of strategy and strategic success. Both influence the making and execution of strategy in multiple ways. Human participants in strategy wear a set of analytical blinders composed of their ideological and cultural assumptions regarding the strategic environment and how to shape it. These blinders are a potential weakness for exploitation by our adversaries and other actors when we wear them, but opportunities for exploitation by us when they are worn by others.[11] The strategist's frame of reference affects how he sees the world and how he advocates interacting within it. These human preferences influence how strategy is constructed and implemented. For example, strategists looking at the world from the perspective of realism, liberalism, or constructivism will have divergent worldviews and will likely arrive at different strategic approaches.[12] Strategists are both aided and limited by these constructs. Such constructs discipline thinking but also potentially limit consideration of alternatives.

Ideology and culture not only shape the expectations and goals of those who formulate and approve strategy but the ferocity and stamina of those who execute it. In addition, ideology and culture influence national popular support and global acceptance of the legitimacy of a national strategy.[13] Consequently, the strategist must consider the cultural and ideological perspectives of strategy internally and externally, as well as personally. Internally there are preferences that garner and sustain acceptability and support, and externally there are differences base on nationality, ideology, religion, and culture that must be considered in the formulation and implementation of strategy. One needs to look no further than the American experience in Vietnam to illustrate this. Once the war was publicly reframed into a nationalist struggle for Vietnamese unity, both domestic and foreign support waned. For Americans, sustainment of a nonrepresentative South Vietnamese government no longer justified the costs in lives on both sides. The strategist must know what motivates him and others, and what meets the criteria of both internal and external acceptability. Strategy founded on false constructs or beliefs, or inconsistent with acceptability criteria at home or abroad, is at greater risk.

Strategy must be consistent with the national values and acceptable to international norms. For the United States, this can be particularly problematic. The United States' liberal culture (free markets, equal opportunity, free elections, liberal democracy, constitutionalism, rule of law, and individualism) fundamentally clashes with many other societies. Cultural conflicts about faith and identity are reflected at the individual and societal levels. As the first universal nation, the modern United States has a distinct culture that does not include to the same degree the elements of hierarchy, community, tradition, and custom so evident in older, more stratified societies. Consequently, U.S. strategy is prone to clash with the elites and populations of non-western cultures and to differ on specific issues even with traditional Europe.[14] Historical experience and outlook differ by nationality and culture, with these differences often posing issues for strategy formulation and execution. It does not follow, however, that the United States must change these elements in other societies; they need only to be recognized and accommodated by strategy. Legitimacy, morality, and cultural appreciation are keys to long-term effective strategy because they address the human dimension of interaction within the strategic environment. Expediency in regard to them may produce short-term gains, but risks alienating too many other actors. In the end, we must learn to see ourselves, our allies, our adversaries, and others as an integral part of strategy.[15] We must understand that "strategy is as much about psychology as it is facts on the ground."[16] Above all, strategy is about seeing the complexity and long-term possibilities inherent in the strategic circumstances.

> As a minimum they [strategists] must see clearly both themselves and potential adversaries, their strengths, weaknesses, preconceptions, and limits— through humility, relentless and historically informed critical analysis, and restless dissatisfaction even in victory. They must weigh imponderables through structured debates that pare away personal, organizational, and national illusions and conceits. They must squarely address issues that are bureaucratic orphans. They must unerringly discern and prepare to strike the enemy jugular—whether by surprise attack or attrition, in war or in political and economic struggle. And in the end, makers of strategy must cheerfully face the uncertainties of decision and the dangers of action.[17]

Strategists must swim in complexity to understand the strategic environment and be open to all its possibilities, while planners seek to simplify and clarify so that they can act directly.[18] These distinct roles call for two different thought processes, but westerners, with their unitary outlooks, are culturally at a disadvantage in perceiving possibilities in the strategic realm.

Western thinking is primarily scientific or Newtonian. To get the rationality of western logic, the reality of the world is expressed in either *or* terms—it is assumed to be either black or white. The strategic environment is much less objective than Western logic portrays it; often containing more gray than black and white. Good strategists have always recognized this ambiguity and how to think about it. It is only recently that a discipline of so-called "fuzzy logic" has emerged to describe the greater complexity and corresponding openness in thinking required of the strategic environment. Fuzzy logic or "fuzzy thinking," however poorly named, helps illuminate the realities of the strategic environment because it provides allowance for degree, probability, and ambiguity in the formulation of objectives and concepts.

The science of fuzzy logic is an attempt to contrast reality with the binary logic inherent to Western scientific thought. Binary logic is rooted in Aristotle's philosophical law that something is either A *or* "not A." It cannot be A *and* "not A." It is either true or false. Thus, in Western science, math, logic, and much of culture, we assume a world of blacks and whites that does not change—this is bivalent logic—two-valuedness. This assumption permeates Western thinking. For example, you are either with us or against us. Every statement is either true or false; it has a truth value of 1 or 0. Thus, if you are asked if a number is a 1 or a 0, it is clearly one or the other. In reality, the world is very much gray. If you are asked if 0.4 is a 1 or a 0, in Western bivalent thinking you must decide which it is and act accordingly. In reality it is more than a 0 and less than a 1, something in between, or gray. Hence, fuzzy logic argues everything is a matter of degree or multivalance—with three or more options or an infinite spectrum of options instead of the two extremes of true or false. Fuzzy logic advocates argue that, for the sake of simplicity, our culture traded off accuracy—the way the world is in reality—for a black or white answer. As a consequence, Western scientific thought is limited or hindered by this bivalent logic. As shown by recent developments, "fuzzy thinking" better reflects reality in both math and science. New "smarter" appliances, computers, and other products are already in the marketplace as a result of the application of this science.[19]

Fuzzy logic also has application in strategy, but scientific or Newtonian thought practices dominate most Western thought. As a result, military planners tend to seek certainty in their planning processes—direct cause and effect—even at the expense of accuracy or reality. In the sense that executors of strategy need to work from facts and concrete assumptions about cause and effect to coordinate and implement their activities, this practice serves organizational planning needs well. But such Newtonian thinking at the strategic levels distorts reality and obscures the actual complexity, leading to faulty assumptions and hiding potential issues and options. Strategic thinking is better served by openness to possibilities rather than a constrained perspective.

Again, Clausewitz recognized the difference in reality and planning with his concept of friction. His cautions that: "The good general must know friction in order to overcome it whenever possible, and in order not to expect a standard of achievement in his operations which this very friction makes impossible."[20] Friction results from what cannot be known, what changes from what you knew, and all those glitches that can beset an operation—the reality of war. Friction at the operational and tactical levels is mitigated by proper planning and appropriate anticipation and reaction—branches and sequels to the plan. In essence, the good general creates a black and white reality by attempting to account for everything possible in the planning process. Since friction affects the enemy army as well as one's own, the commander who creates reality best is at an advantage in overcoming friction and winning the engagement.[21] At the strategic level, the degree of uncertainty and complexity is much greater because of the scope of time and nature of the environment. The future cannot be predicted with sufficient precision because the "frictions" are too great to plan for successfully. Good strategy is designed to accommodate, deter, and seek advantages in the realities of degree, probability, and ambiguity—all incident to a complex chaotic system. It accommodates and uses friction. Fuzzy logic helps to explain the ambiguity and uncertainty observed at this level—revealing more of the possibilities to the strategist, while at the same time qualifying expectations. The future is shaped from the structuring of these "possibilities" and expectations into a coherent strategy, expressed as ends, ways, and means, leading to a better end-state.

Since strategy can be formulated at different levels, the strategist should be clear in regard to the level at which he is working even as he remains holistic in his outlook. At the national level, strategy is concerned with maintaining internal systems in balance with one another, while creating effects in the external environment that favor the state over time. When it focuses on lower levels or specific issues, strategy is really a case of particular generalization—what strategic effect is required to what purpose and how does it affect the whole of the environment. On the other hand, strategy at any level is not problem solving in a classic sense. It does not seek to solve a specific problem as much as to anticipate a future and shape an environment in which fewer problems arise and those that do can be resolve in favorable terms. Causation in strategy is contingent, not categorical. Context always matters. Ultimately the success of strategic effects depends on what the adversary and others chose to do and on what reality turns out to be. Hence, strategists must cultivate a web-like sense of reality, seeing everything as connected in some way to everything else and being open to all possibilities. The strategist provides direction that is consistent with the past as it bridges to the future.[22] In this process, strategy must be inherently flexible as it anticipates the future. Thus, strategy is always seeking a balance between specificity and flexibility in establishing boundaries for planning. Strategy

Figure 5.1 Strategy and Favorable Strategic Effects.

does not dictate the future, but it does anticipate it and seeks to shape it in favorable terms at whatever level it functions, maintaining an appropriate degree of adaptability and flexibility.

The true purpose of strategy is to create favorable effects in support of policy goals for the advancement or protection of national interests. This relationship is depicted in Figure 5.1. Strategic effects are the impact that *the accomplishment* of strategic objectives has on the environment. Effect follows from strategic performance—the synergy of the objective(s) achieved, the concept(s) employed, and the resources used. Thus, strategic performance is the measure of the quality of actions actually executed to achieve the policy aims.[23] Effects occur on different levels and from different causes within the environment. Effects must be comprehended in at least three dimensions. First, good strategy deliberately seeks to create multiorder effects—a chain of effects that culminates in strategic-level success. Such intended first-, second- and third-order effects, etc., are a rational product of the strategist's thinking, with the purpose of stimulating and influencing interaction or conditions within the environment in favor of the policy aims. When a strategic concept is implemented to achieve an objective that produces an intended reaction from the adversary or a direct change within the environment—a first-order effect is created. But if the strategist has foreseen and sought multiordered effects as a result of the concept in action, he has deliberately created cascading effects—intended second- and third-order effects. On the other hand, a different dimension of effects unfolds when the strategist fails to fully comprehend the consequences of his choices, with the strategy creating unanticipated consequences in the environment. A third dimension of effects that must be considered is the intervention of chance or adversaries and others in reacting to the effects of the original strategy. The good strategist seeks to understand all these dimensions of effects and capitalize on or compensate for them in his strategy. Thus, he prepares for those effects he foresees and maintains a degree of adaptability and flexibility for those he cannot foresee. Fuzzy thinking helps the strategist to understand the possible manifestations of effects by revealing the shades of reality.

Ultimately the role of the strategist is to evaluate the complex and evolving environment and translate policy goals into terms from which planning can proceed. Strategic thinking must see the environment as it actually is, identify the factors that favor or hinder the policy aims, and anticipate the possibilities for achievement of policy goals. The strategist is concerned with facts, factors, and assumptions in this process. Each must be right. Facts are reality as it is—the grayness of fuzzy thinking as opposed to invariable black and white. Factors are facts that affect policy aims. Assumptions bridge the unknown. Through the formulation of appropriate ends, ways, and means to manipulate the factors and take advantage of the possibilities, the strategist creates favorable effects on behalf of policy goals. Openness and recognition of personal biases and preferences move the strategist closer to a proper assessment of reality. This assessment tempered by an appreciation of chance and others' ideological and cultural biases and preferences—in light of interests and policy goals—defines the effects desired. A proper mind-set on the part of the strategist is critical to the development of good strategy.

STRATEGY IS NOT PLANNING

Military professionals, in particular, come from a world of very adept planners; they learn planning methodologies from the day they enter service. Effective problem solving and planning abilities are also keys to success among other national security professionals. *Strategy is not planning.* As described above, it partakes of a different mind-set. Planning makes strategy actionable. It relies on a high degree of certainty—a world that is concrete and can be addressed in explicit terms. In essence it takes a gray world and makes it black and white through its analysis of the facts and assumptions about the unknown. Planning is essentially linear and deterministic, focusing heavily on first-order cause and effect. It assumes that the future results can be precisely known if enough is known about the facts and the conditions affecting the undertaking. The planning process is essential to reduce uncertainty at the operational and tactical levels—it allows detailed actions to be prescribed. In reality, uncertainty can never quite be achieved even at that level, and it increases exponentially as we ascend from the tactical to the operational to the strategic level. The planning process works because the lower the level, the more limited the scope and complexity and the shorter the timeline; hence the amount of unknowns are limited and can be compensated for in branches and sequels to create enough "certainty." *Planning is not strategy*. It is essential for the successful execution of a strategy—making strategy actionable, but requires a different mind-set. Most national security professionals are *trained* for the certainty of planning throughout their career, but must be *educated* for uncertainty as they enter the strategic realm.

The strategist must understand the difference between strategy and planning in order to produce good strategy. The planner must understand the difference between planning and strategy in order to implement strategy successfully. Planning bridges the gap between strategy and execution. The purpose of planning is to create certainty so that people and organizations can act. The purpose of strategy formulation is to clarify, influence, manage, or resolve the VUCA of the strategic environment through the identification and creation of strategic effects in support of policy goals. Strategy lays down what is important and to be achieved, sets the parameters for the necessary actions, and prescribes what the state is willing to allocate in terms of resources. Thus, strategy, through its hierarchal nature, identifies the objectives to be achieved and defines the box in which detailed planning can be accomplished—it bounds planning. Within that box, planning adapts strategy to a concrete world with facts, figures, and interrelated and sequenced actions calculated to achieve the strategy's objectives. The planner is Newtonian or scientific in his approach; the strategist is more "fuzzy." Both share the paradigm of ends, ways, and means. Too many in the national security community confuse strategy and planning. As a consequence, planning-level thinking is often applied in the strategy-development process or planning objectives and concepts are elevated to the strategic level. When this occurs, even though the plan may be successful, the resulting strategic effects fail to adequately support, or are actually counterproductive to, the stated policy goals or other interests.

CONCLUSION

Strategic theory and thinking are applicable to all national security community members working with policy and strategy. Both policy and strategy formulation and implementation are enhanced by a thorough grounding in theory and practice. From this grounding the professional develops a strategic mind-set that enables him to comprehend and influence the VUCA of the strategic environment through the creation of judicious effects. Strategy bounds planning with its articulation of ends, ways, and means, creating the problem to be solved, and framing a degree of certainty for planning. Planning achieves the strategic objective through disciplined planning processes and the resultant actions. Strategy deals with uncertainty, planning deals with certainty. Both are valid and essential disciplined thought processes.

6

The International Environment

One country may support another's cause, but will never take it so seriously as it takes its own.[1]

—Clausewitz

Typically in the study of international relations the international system has meant the existing international order of state and nonstate actors, the power relationships among them, and the agreements, institutions, and accepted practices that govern their interactions. The strategist and other national security professionals make use of this field of study, but their concern is the whole of the international environment—both its physical and nonphysical attributes. The international environment is that part of the strategic environment that is beyond the state's own domestic environment and the place where the state and all of its attributes interact with the rest of the world. The domestic environment consists of the internal physical and humanistic systems that define what the state is and how it may choose or must act within the greater environment. Each state or system in the strategic environment has this internal environment that must interact with those systems external to it. Taken together, the domestic and international environments constitute the whole of the strategic environment and are one representation of its internal–external dialectic that leads to multiordered effects. Understanding the international environment is important because the United States is interconnected with the rest of the world. For example, just the State Department listing of agreements and treaties—not the documents themselves—is over 600 pages.[2] This chapter examines the international environment as a system of systems and the implications for policy and strategy formulation.

How to conceptualize and evaluate the international environment is a challenging task. In *Games Nations Play* the authors use three levels of analysis to do this: the international system level, the actor level, and the decision-making level.[3] This is a commonly accepted model for explaining interaction within the environment, having withstood the test of time in educating thousands of students in international relations. The international system and international actors are addressed in this chapter. The decision-making level is addressed, and further developed, along with the other various domestic factors that affect policy and strategy formulation in the following chapter on the domestic environment. The position taken herein accepts the usefulness of the levels of analysis model and adds to it, bringing in ideas from other theorists and practices. Again, theorists have given us knowledge and insights into how to conceptualize the international environment, and how it and its subsystems interact, but the national security professional must assess it in his own time and for his own purposes. Therefore, theory again serves as a guide to the proper questions, but does not provide specific answers.

PHYSICAL ATTRIBUTES

The international environment has both physical and nonphysical spheres. It functions as a system of systems and chaos theory and chance are at work in both spheres. Geography, natural resources, weather, the physical existence of peoples and structures, and physics are all physical attributes of this environment. Strategists and others must take account of these physical systems. Physical systems are to some degree simpler and easier to understand than humanistic systems of international and domestic politics, economics, militaries, and collective mentalities, but they possess their own VUCA (volatility, uncertainty, complexity, and ambiguity). Weather is an obvious example. While modern science has made great progress in predicting weather and to a lesser degree other natural events, a degree of unpredictability still exists. Less obvious is the contextual relationship of the physical attributes of the environment and policy and strategy. For example, a large underemployed population in another part of the world can be an advantage if your economy needs labor and you can access it competitively. On the other hand, it is a disadvantage if your internal population is underemployed and others are taking advantage of the same labor to undercut your production costs. Likewise, the Dardanelles strait is an advantage if you want to preclude access to the Mediterranean Sea from the Black Sea, but might prove a significant disadvantage if someone contested your access to the Black Sea from the Mediterranean.

The physical attributes of the international environment are often easier to determine than the humanistic ones, but their value is always related to the context of the interest and the opportunity, challenge, or threat that policy or strategy seeks to take advantage of or overcome. The humanistic systems that govern international relations and politics can have effects in the physical environment. For example, bilateral or international agreements can govern labor practices and production or make the Dardanelles an international waterway. In a similar manner, changes in technology and economics can give new meaning to geography and strategy. The need for coaling stations for ships driven by steam instead of wind increased the strategic value of Pacific islands in the late nineteenth century. Today, the incessant demand for oil makes the oil-rich states of the Middle East international players and of grave strategic concern to most developed nations. Air travel and the Internet have bridged many of the time and space limitations of the early twentieth century that limited globalization, but have brought new issues. Hence, the strategist must see the physical world as it is, as it might be, and in the context of the interests and issues he is working. Policy and strategy must adhere to the laws of the physical universe in the service of the state but such laws have meaning in the context of the nature of a changing environment and interests and issues.

INTERNATIONAL RELATIONS

Historically, states have been considered the major actors in the international environment, but state roles and power are increasingly challenged or supplemented by nonstate actors. Nonetheless, to understand the role of actors in general the state remains the primary starting place. The fundamental roles of a state are to provide for the security and well-being of its people. States vary in their definitions of what constitutes security and well-being within their own borders. States also fulfill these roles with varying degrees of success. Some states fall short by choice, but more often failure is a result of inability or indifference. In the international environment these roles are pursued in the context of the existence of other states and nonstate actors, each seeking ways to serve its interests in security and well-being. Exactly how states do this and how the international system functions, or more precisely, "how states should do this and how the international system must function," is a matter of open debate among theorists. It is debatable because there is a degree of truth and intellectual value in each of the theories in understanding the international order. Consequently, each theory provides insights into international order and how it functions that are useful, but none explains it completely. Scholars have subdivided these theories into numerous schools by how theorists approach the study, nuances in the explanations, and the facts or relationships that are their primary focus. The basic schools of realism, idealism, liberal institutionalism, and constructivism differentiate the primary perspectives for viewing international politics even though there are numerous others. Taken together they serve as lenses into the international order to understand how it acts and reacts, and suggest how it can be influenced and shaped.[4]

Realism as a theory was initially proposed by Hans Morgenthau in *Politics Among Nations* (1948). Some of its premises are evident in Thucydides' *History of the Peloponnesian War*, Machiavelli's *The Prince and Discourses*, and Thomas Hobbes' *The Leviathan*, but Morgenthau's specific purpose was to provide a rational explanation of the behavior of states and the international order—international politics. He saw international politics as a struggle for power and states as the main actors. He argued people have an insatiable desire for power and in international politics, no matter what the stated aim, it is ultimately always about gaining power. The reality, he argued, is that this human desire manifests itself in state ambitions that cannot be appeased and management of the international system had to be rooted in an appreciation for national interests. According to realists peace is preserved by the maintenance of a balance of power among the states.[5]

Morgenthau's focus on the realism of power was refined and surpassed by Kenneth Waltz's neo-realist explanation in *Theory of International Politics* (1979). Waltz rejected human nature as the core justification and argued from a structural perspective. The fundamental problem as he saw it was the basic fact that in international existence there were no central authoritative international organizations to make and enforce rules or provide order. Consequently, the international environment is one of anarchy and power politics are the rule. States are the primary actors, and they decide what their interests are and how to pursue them. Each state is concerned primarily with its own interests and can ultimately rely only on itself for survival. Each state has military power, and since other states cannot be fully trusted and there is nothing else, force or the threat of force becomes the ultimate arbiter. In this environment all states feel insecure, and the increase of capability by one state to enhance its security automatically increases the insecurity of the others to some degree—the security dilemma.[6]

On the surface realism describes the international environment in terms of win–lose. However, this is hardly the case when studied in detail and collectively realists offer the strategic thinker much to ponder. Waltz argued that power was not the end itself, but the means by which states sought their true end, which is security. Waltz also recognized the international environment was a complex system, and as such, impersonal forces—structure, anarchy, and distribution of power—influenced state behavior. Hence, states seek security through international structure and power. This pursuit makes the achievement of a balance of power to enhance relative stability an almost automatic result as states align among themselves to ensure their survival and prevent any one state from becoming too powerful. The realists' perspectives on the role of power, the nature of the international environment, and the interaction of states offer key insights into the international system. However, their theory is only one point of view and misses other key aspects that also help define the international environment.[7]

Early idealism, sometimes referred to as utopianism, was an interwar reaction to the secret diplomacy and slaughter of World War I. Woodrow Wilson is often considered the intellectual father of the school, but idealism is an intellectual descendant of classic liberalism. Idealists rejected war as a necessary solution to international issues. They argued that people are basically good and act ethically, if left to their natural inclinations. Believing people act rationally and are capable of controlling their own destinies, they favored democratic governments and state decisions arrived at openly. To idealists there is a natural harmony of interests among states and all share the interest of peace. Nations that sought war were both irrational and immoral. In their view nations that worked together could resolve any issue without force. According to Wilson, world security would be achieved through democratic ideas, self-determination and international venues for free trade, and peaceful settlement of disputes. The terms imposed at Versailles and the resulting World War II proved the idealists optimistic, but the ideas persist because they appeal to the values of many.[8]

Realism and idealism as theories were integrated in liberal institutionalism. Liberal institutionalism accepts the realist position that states are rational actors and pursue interests based on cost-benefit analysis. E.H. Carr in *The Twenty-Years Crisis, 1919–1939* (1939) proposed that international stability resulted from both power and legitimacy. This idea was further developed in several books in the 1970s when others argued that states will forego competition if they perceive greater gain through cooperation. However, to forego the competitive use of power, they must be assured that other states will not cheat and gain advantage. To ensure "fair play," and hence security, institutionalists argue the solution is through use of international institutions to resolve issues and ensure fairness. From their perspective, it is not the inherent anarchy of the international system that controls behavior but the decisions of domestic political institutions that lead to a preference for cooperation across the spectrum of power as opposed to a narrowly defined physical security provided by military power. "Democracies do not make war on each other" is one extension of this logic.[9]

Some in the institutionalist school see the role of institutions as transforming the anarchy of the international system into a constitutional order with international and legal and political institutions allocating rights and limiting the exercise of power by states. In their view tensions in the environment are created by the dynamics of changing power distributions as one state experiences internal growth that increases its power relative to others. In a purely realist model, at some point the rising state's power would be checked by another individual power or through the creation of a balance with alliances, eventually resulting in war and the determination of the dominant power. Yet, the calculation of the rising power is affected by the status quo—the institutions, laws, and practices that govern international politics and reward and punish. If these are perceived to be legitimate and favorable, they argue, a rising power has little reason to challenge the dominant power or existing power system.[10]

One more major school that merits consideration is constructivism. Sometimes also referred to as idealists, constructivists argue that state interests are derived from ideas and norms. They argue there are no permanent state interests and the anarchy of international politics is what states make it. Hence anarchy is tamed through the construction of international institutions and practices that are socially constructed by states at various times to resolve issues. Over time these become the norm of acceptable behavior and legitimate states adhere to them. In addition, they believe the state's identity and how it perceives others shapes its interests. They view the state as a social being and much of its identity as a social construct. Consequently, how a state sees itself is how it acts out its interests in relation to others. For example, if it sees itself as peace loving, its interests and the pursuit of them will be shaped by this.[11]

Theories of international relations or politics help to organize, interpret, and predict to some degree the reality of the international environment. It is not that anyone of these basic theories, or the numerous variations of them and other theories, are correct in an absolute sense—indeed, all of them offer valid perspectives, but fail individually to account for all international behavior and what motivates populations, politicians, states, and other actors. What matters is that taken collectively they provide lenses from which the strategist and others can evaluate the chaos of the international system and help identify potential strategic factors on which to base policy and strategy.

STRUCTURE AND STABILITY

Theorists disagree about the nature of the relationship between stability and structure in the international environment. A stable international environment can generally be defined as a lack of major wars, minimal violence and peaceful settlement of most differences, and a desire to continue the current system. Such a description allows for most interaction among states and other actors, including the possibility of war. An unstable system is prone to major violence, lives with the threat of a predominant single power, and poses risk to the survival of most member states. Hence, stability in the international environment is really about the balanced distribution of power. How power is distributed—structure—conditions international behavior. Since most power resides in states, realists argue the number of major powers and how power is distributed among them determines structure.[12] Others argue, it is not how power is distributed but how power is managed.

Realism portrays the international system as potentially existing in four states: anarchy, unipolarity, bipolarity, and multipolarity. Anarchy is the natural state, unrestrained by order. In a unipolar system, one state or coalition is dominant and can impose its will on the other states. While it does possess one of the characteristics of instability, such a system is stable as long as the hegemonic state can suppress violence and control the aspirations of other states or would-be states. Bipolar systems have two superpowers or coalitions who have an equivalent balance of power. Today, in the face of modern terrorism, rogue states, and weapons of mass destruction (WMD), some look longingly at the bipolar Cold War as a very stable world order. In their view, the near equal distribution of nuclear military power between the USSR and the United States created a bipolar world in which the two superpowers successfully managed stability in order to survive. However, it can also be argued that the Cold War bipolar system was inherently unstable because the two superpowers continuously sought advantages through arms races and proxy wars in order keep one or the other from gaining hegemony.[13]

An ideal multipolar system would have five or more equivalent great powers. Some theorists argue, it is inherently more stable because of its complexity and flexibility. In such an international system states can align or realign themselves to sustain a balance, and the balance restrains destabilizing behavior and precludes the rise of a hegemonic power. Balance exists because rising power begets countervailing power in other states in order to serve two key purposes: preservation of the security of each individual state and protection of the international system as a whole. Realists argue peace is more likely when an appropriate balance has been achieved. However, they point out that in practice peace is a lesser objective of countervailing power—sustaining the balance is worth war, because without it there is no guarantee of security or an international order in which a state can pursue its interests independent of hegemony. Hence, lesser states perceive sustaining a balance as both a requirement of security and as creating opportunities to pursue state interests. For example, this logic offers one explanation for why France and Russia chose to align in the United Nations Security Council against the United States, the lone superpower, on the invasion of Iraq. The counter to this stability argument is that the constant realignment creates uncertainty and contributes to miscalculations in policy leading to major wars.[14]

Liberal institutionalism and constructivism suggest another basis of international order. Coming from slightly different perspectives, they both see a stable order flowing from the construction of international legal, political, and social institutions that facilitate the growing interdependency among the states and among the states' populations. Interdependency is an important phenomenon in the current globalization.[15] A counter to this argument is that interdependency, like modernity, creates its own issues and these may well result in conflict. In addition, such a structure would require the major state actors to relinquish a part of their power—something major powers are particularly reluctant to do.

When pursuing interests within the international environment, states may choose to act unilaterally, bilaterally, or multilaterally in a domain of concern. These choices create structure within the international order, some ad hoc, such as coalitions, and some more permanent, such as alliances. This structure will invariably be at least three-sided—the two protagonists and all others. Consequently, there are advantages and disadvantages to each method of acting. Unilateralism gives the state the most control over its strategy and actions, but raises concerns among other states about hegemonic ambitions and stability. Bilateral action requires the state to negotiate ends, ways, and means with one other power, limiting to some degree flexibility and freedom of action. Multilateralism is also an official government-to-government relationship, but with three or more other countries. It makes each state accountable to one another for their specific actions in the particular domain of concern of the group. Obviously it places greater limitations on flexibility and freedom of action by requiring the sharing of authority with others who may not have the same priorities, inhibiting timely and efficient action, complicating secrecy, politicizing issues related to ends and ways, and complicating subordinate plans and efforts. Nonetheless, bilateralism and multilateralism have appeal because they provide legitimacy, influence over others, additional capabilities and resources, and physical access.[16] They also often allay fears in regard to hegemony, because they place constraints on stronger powers. Consequently, use of bilateral and multilateral structures has appeal to both weak and strong states. The choice becomes part of the strategic calculation.

THE ACTORS

Within the international system a number of actors interact. The primary and most powerful actor is the state. The state's power is based on sovereignty, which was codified in the Peace of Westphalia in 1648 and led to the modern state system. Power is unequally balanced among state actors and this contributes to a fundamental security dilemma of how to ensure the right to sovereignty. While the form of the state has varied greatly over time and exists in various forms today, its validity still rests on the principles of sovereignty. Sovereignty has two key aspects. First, the state, no matter its form of government, accepts no internal equals within its territory. Second, the state accepts no external power as the ultimate authority within its territory. Sovereignty gives the government of the state the authority to control its populations, regulate commerce, distribute wealth, raise militaries, dispense justice, and define relations with the rest of the international environment for all its citizens. It is in effect a long-standing agreement among states to live and let live. More recently, native populations and an emerging global civil society have interpreted the primary role of government to be to provide adequately for its people. Sovereignty as a practical concept has always been problematic because of issues of authority and power in both the domestic and international environments, but it cannot be easily discarded or modified because the legitimacy of state power internally and externally is based on it.[17]

States are more than territory. They consist of populations, resources, social order and structure, values and ideologies, cultural and sub-cultural identities—as well as strategic cultures—and interdependent relationships with other states and actors. These all affect how states act and their success. States, or more precisely governments, that cannot maintain internal and external legitimacy or properly develop and exercise power internally and externally, ultimately fail. Failed states are problematic for all states because they threaten the stability of the international order. Internal legitimacy refers to the state's ability to provide for its population in terms of security and social justice. While a state's power can provide security and deny social justice for long periods of time and still remain internally stable, the modern trend favors states with an acceptable degree of social justice. This trend is reinforced by the exchange of information in the global world order and the pressures generated by the international community itself for greater social justice. Internal power is also problematic when it is misapplied or insufficient. Not only can people rise and change their government for failing to provide security or social justice, but a strong leader, cabal, or insurgency can overthrow legitimate authority by promising a better future. Externally, the international community and individual states demonstrate an increasing proclivity to intervene in other state's internal issues because the problems are spilling over or the humanitarian consequences of internal issues of failure are too great. And, of course, as Iraq's invasion of Kuwait in 1990 demonstrated, the old fashion power grab is not out of fashion. All of these pose issues for international order.[18]

Current states can be conceptualized as being one of four different kinds to include authoritarian, democratic, revolutionary, and failed states. Authoritarian states are very hierarchical and maintain strict social control over their populations. In these states the elites use oppressive state authority to stay in power and reap the benefits of society. Such states openly adhere to the tenets of international order as long as it serves their purposes and does not threaten the elites in control. While they may take opportunistic advantage of war, it is always calculated in regard to retaining power. Democratic states have more civil liberties and freedom and are responsive to the desires and opinions of their populations. Social justice is greater and the authorities can be challenged in court and through elections. Such states generally embrace the international order and attempt to encourage it toward more democratic values in regard to free trade, rule of law, and human rights because they see this as benefiting their citizens' well-being. Democratic states are reluctant to go to war unless provoked, but human rights can be a provocation. Revolutionary states reject the existing international order and the prevailing political, economic, and cultural system that perpetuates it. Their internal unity and motivation comes from their ideology that promises a better world. Such states are more likely to resort to war because they continually feel threatened and they resent the existence of other forms of states. While they reject the existing international order, they use it as a protective shield and to enhance their power whenever possible. The rogue state can be seen as a variation of the revolutionary state, motivated not by an ideology but by the fears or ambitions of a charismatic leader or other power elites. Failed states are the fourth kind of state. These states are failed because they cannot provide for the security and well-being of their populations. As a result, they are taken advantage of by other states or exploited by nonstate actors for purposes that invariably pose issues for the stability of the international environment. Sovereignty continues to have value for all states because it empowers and protects states as actors at home and in the international order.

A popular theme in some current literature is the demise of the state system as a result of globalization and the rise of nonstate actors. Such an anticipatory premise needs to be dispelled. Modernity and globalization have resulted in the expansion of private and supra-state economic, legal, and social organizations and activities whose very existence violates a strict interpretation of sovereignty. Yet, their existence is a reflection of the waiving of some aspects of sovereignty by states for perceived advantages. It is even probable that these organizations' activities will contribute in part to additional failed states as their interventions reveal internal contradictions within states in regard to economics and social justice or expose destabilizing ambition on the part of some states. However they have changed over the centuries, states have proved to be remarkably viable institutions. Bruce D. Porter in *War and the Rise of the State* (1994) concludes that those that are eager to report the demise of the state fail to realize why it has been so successful—its ability to adapt, raise revenues, organize people and resources, and use the military element of power.[19]

Other actors exist in the international system. Referred to generally as nonstate actors, they fall into several categories. Voluntary associations of sovereign states that join together in formal structures for various purposes are called intergovernmental organizations (IGOs). While such organizations may have extensive bureaucracies for administration and operations, decisions are negotiated by each state's assigned representative to the organization. As such they are extensions of collective state power, and states participate because it is perceived to be in their overall interest. The existence of IGOs demonstrates the possibility of common interests and a need for common endeavors. IGOs can be used as instruments by the policymaker or strategist, or they may have to be accounted for by a particular policy or strategy. They can help resolve issues, but in some cases may contribute to them. When supportive, they bring legitimacy, alternative options, and resources.

Intergovernmental organizations' memberships may be regional or global. They may focus on specific functions or be more comprehensive in nature. The United Nations (UN) is the largest and best-known IGO. It seeks to get all states to participate and can be comprehensive in the issues it addresses. Other examples of global IGOs include the World Bank (WB), International Monetary Fund (IMF), and the General Agreement on Tariffs and Trade (GATT). These are more functional oriented, and membership is less universal than in the UN. Many more IGOs are regional and seek to promote cooperation or resolve issues on a regional basis. For example, the Organization of American States cooperates on a variety of issues affecting the western hemisphere. The Asia-Pacific Economic Council (APEC) includes Asian and western hemisphere nations cooperating on economic issues. IGOs also break down into sub-regional groups. The Gulf Cooperation Council is an IGO of six Arab states cooperating in common defense; a military alliance like North Atlantic Treaty Organization (NATO). Such organizations have a collective power and often have bureaucracies that possess a degree of power and pursue internal agendas. The very existence of IGOs makes them actors to be considered as part of the interaction of the international environment.

Supranational actors are created when states forego some of their autonomy by transferring some parts of sovereignty to an IGO. Such is the case with the European Union (EU), in which states signing the Treaty on European Union agreed to empower the EU to foster common foreign policy and security positions for the member states. A second treaty created a common EU currency. Yet, in this case the member states retained the fundamental decision-making authority in their own hands by the way the treaty was structured.[20] The United States submits to some form of international jurisdiction in over 112 treaties, most of which are commercial, including the World Trade Organization (WTO) and the North American Free Trade Agreement.

Other categories of nonstate actors include multinational corporations (MNCs), nongovernmental organizations (NGOs), and other transnational actors. Unlike IGOs, these actors are not organs of states. Such nonstate actors represent an unprecedented rise of civil society into the international arena. These actors pursue their own interests, although they may work in collaboration with states, IGOs, or other actors. All transnational actors are defined as having their headquarters in one state and centrally directed operations in two or more states. While IGOs require agreement among states, transnational actors require only access to states. The access requirement places external constraints on these actors, but states have no direct control within these nongovernmental organizations. They are transnational because they seek to operate without regard to borders.[21] Because transnational actors can be labeled in terms of good and evil, how they are referred to becomes important. Hence, while all are transnational and nongovernmental, the common usage refers to multinational corporations, nongovernmental organizations, and other transnational actors.

Multinational corporations are the most numerous and widely diverse NGOs. The sheer size and global reach of some of the MNCs make them increasingly significant internationally. Many have resources that exceed those of most of the small states they do business in and operate over areas that represent global economic empires. Taken together, they are part of the economic glue that binds the global economy together, and they exert individual and collective influence in the international environment by the economic decisions they make and their relationships with the domestic elites. How much and what kind of influence varies greatly from case to case, but there is growing concern among some that their economic power is being translated into political power within states and they are increasingly seeking to shape an international environment favorable to themselves without regard to states and others.[22] Some MNCs do have access to military or hard power through contracting or influence within state governments. However valid this concern is in regard to specific MNCs, the MNCs' role in creating and operating a global economy generally raises the global standard of living and creates interdependency within the international environment.

Transnational religious, humanitarian, social, and professional organizations are commonly referred to as international NGOs. The *Yearbook of International Organization* lists more than 25,000 NGOs. The Roman Catholic Church is considered by some as a religious NGO, although in some respects it has aspects of a state. Other religions have their international organizations and affiliations that give them a voice in the international environment. The International Committee of the Red Cross is a well-known humanitarian NGO that has as stated purposes the protection of lives and dignity of victims of war and internal violence and to provide them with assistance. The Geneva Conventions originated with this movement and recognize the right of the organization to offer its impartial services. It publishes influential reports on a wide range of humanitarian issues. Other NGOs also operate and exert influence in both the domestic and international environments. Amnesty International and Doctors Without Borders demonstrate how professions and other like-minded groups influence the strategic environment through activities as an NGO.[23] Such organizations create international credibility on certain issues that gives them moral legitimacy, and therefore influence. They have a constituency among the world's population, particularly with opinion shapers, and bring both capability and resources to the table. While they may cooperate with states, lending their influence and capabilities and resources, they are independent actors and may choose to go their own way. In fact, many of these organizations choose not to associate with state actors or their agents beyond United Nations' registration because they believe it affects their independence and credibility. Some also use the moral legitimacy gained through their altruistic advocacy on one type of issue to shape opinions on other issues.[24]

The organizations and groups most often labeled as transnational actors, or sometimes "other transnational actors," are those whom the international order considers illegal or on the fringe of legality. Distinctions among these groups are also useful. National liberation organizations (NLOs) are insurgencies that represent "states in waiting." Nationalism is their primary appeal and they seek to liberate "territory" claimed by current regimes and take on the mantle of states. Such organizations are considered illegal in the threatened state by authorities but may be considered legitimate by parts of the population or parts of the international community. They achieve their transnational character by the popular, special interest, and other state support they receive from other actors in the international environment whether in funding, legitimacy, arms, freedom of movement, favorable support in international forums, or direct military aid. National liberation organizations create their legitimacy by the appeal and recognition of their cause and their focus on creating a nation-state.[25]

Terrorist organizations are also transnational actors and in many respects resemble the NLOs, but differ in purpose and scale of means. NLOs' nationalism generally confines their use of violence internally toward the existing government or occupying power. While using terror as a tactic, their focus is on defeating the "oppressive" government. Terrorist organizations use terror as an escalatory strategy focused on the political will of local and global populations and international, as well as internal state, political leadership. It draws attention to their ideology, which is often perverted and usually lacks any popular appeal until the use of terror focuses attention on their existence and provides an opportunity to attract an audience. With an audience, they can articulate the injustices of the current order and achieve a degree of legitimacy as spokesmen for the oppressed, but unlike NLOs their proposed solutions lack political practicality. Hence, terror compels and sustains their relevance. Terror therefore serves well on one level as a recruiting tool among the like-minded and those frustrated by perceived injustices of the current order, but since the ideology leads to no real end, it can only support a limited organization and attract a limited number of foot soldiers. Terror remains their basis of credibility because it is the only way to demonstrate their ability to act and thus sustain themselves.

Since terror is an escalatory strategy, if their demands are not met, terrorist organizations expand the scope of the terror in the number of casualties, the means of attack, and who is attacked. The greater scope is justified by an internal logic of the ends justifies the means, and a strategic logic of enough terror can cause publics around the world to call for their demands to be accommodated. The NLO poses little threat to the greater international order unless a significant number of states choose to take sides. Terrorists pose a direct threat to the international order because their success is directly linked to escalating and exporting terror, taking advantage of the international order's modernity to leverage public will in their favor. In the process they challenge the existing international order's credibility and stability. Terrorists use ungoverned spaces as safe havens, but NLOs govern or impose shadow governments in their own country even while operating from sanctuaries. Success for both NLOs and terrorist organizations is dependent to some degree on external state support, even if it is nothing more than acquiescence.

Criminal organizations that have operations in multiple countries or achieve the same effects through affiliations are also labeled transnational actors. Motivated largely by personal profit, such actor organizations operate economically much like MNCs but are not constrained by regulatory law. Such organizations may establish safe havens, use violence, and control territory within state boundaries. They may also control or exert great influence over the apparatus of states through payoffs or coercion in order to create these safe havens or favorable "business" climates. At a certain point, such activities subvert the legitimacy of the government and the consequences of the corruption threaten or cause a failed state. Violence is an inherent part of their practice, but they also make use of the advantages of modernity and globalization for illegal activities and often hide behind legitimate businesses to laundry profits.

While it is useful analytically to distinguish among NLOs, terrorists, and criminal actors for strategic understanding and insights, there is an increasing trend where the groups have merged or adopted each other's practices. Consequently, terrorist organizations or NLOs are increasingly turning to crime—drugs, kidnappings, extortion, and robbery on a large scale—to finance their operations, and crime organizations are collaborating with terrorists and NLOs for profit or reciprocal access and protection. The full impact of this morphing and collaboration is unknown, but clearly competitive and corruptive forces are at work and pose a threat to selected states and the current international order.[26]

There are other ways to conceptualize international actors that are helpful to the strategist, but the model of states, IGOs, MNCs, NGOs, and other transnational actors sufficiently conveys the complexity of actors within the international environment. Here, returning to the schools of international relations provides perspective. Realism is correct to argue that states are the primary actors and that power relationships among them matter. On the other hand as liberal institutionalis points out, the increased complexity of the international order, summarized as globalization, makes it more important for individual states to enter IGOs to remain economically viable and to peacefully resolve security issues. Globalization also empowers other actors, either because states see advantages to them or in the current environment they are able to create and sustain a lesser but advantageous role of power for themselves. As with IGOs, most NGOs and MNCs have legitimate and useful roles in the global society. However, the selfish interests and weaknesses of individual states and the seams in international order among states allow bad transnational actors to flourish, and ultimately this threatens the stability of the current order.

The complexity of the current international environment offers opportunities, challenges, and threats to all the actors. Some states will become dysfunctional and fail. Others will join together in agreements that balance power or resolve power issues through negotiation and collaboration. Some states will see advantage in ceding some aspects or level of sovereignty to existing IGOs or merger into larger state-like entities. However, it is unlikely that states, which control the predominance of the natural and social determinants of power, will forego their current positions peacefully. Consequently, states will remain the arbiters of the international order and their choices will continue to dictate its degree of stability. Other actors may take legal advantage of the order, improve on and shape the order, find advantage in the seams among states and within the order, or challenge and corrupt the order to some degree, but only states themselves can sustain or destroy the order by their use, misuse or nonuse of power. States are the final arbiters of power in the international environment and the policymaker and strategist must acknowledge this even as policy and strategy focuses on issues with other actors.

POWER AND INSTRUMENTS OF POWER

Power in the international system can be defined simply as the ability to influence the behavior of other actors in support of your interests. It can be applied in various forms: brute force, coercion, inducement, persuasion, and attraction. Power is the means to get the outcomes the state desires. How power works is not understood very well. Historically, power has generally equated to military might, because military force has been the final arbiter in the state system for 350 years. However, all states and actors possess some form of power or they would not exist. While military force still plays a vital role in today's international environment, other elements and instruments of power have become increasingly important. For example, success in the war on terror depends on strategic communications and economics as well as military power. There is objective power, what a state actually possesses—and subjective power, what others believe a state possesses. There is hard power and soft power; the first is focused on coercion and the second on attraction. Power is relative, not absolute. It is relative to the power possessed by others and to one's willingness to use it. Power has tangible and intangible aspects. Large military forces are a tangible aspect, but the will to use them is intangible. Power is dynamic. States gain and lose power, and gain and lose credibility in regard to the use of power. Power is also contextual. To a large extent the circumstances define the appropriateness of power and its use. The examination and weighing of information in regard to strategic circumstances and power reveal relevant strategic factors and suggest which are key to successful policy and strategy.[27] Again, the strategist and other national security professionals must consider power from the multiple perspectives of self, adversaries, others, the physical world, and chance.[28]

The power of a state can be approached from the perspective of its elements and instruments of power. Elements of power consist of natural determinants and social determinants of power. Natural determinants are categorized as geography, population, and natural resources. Social determinants are categorized as economic, military, political, and socio-psychological. Elements of power measure a nation's capacity to do something and are a measure of potential power. Instruments of power are tools that can be applied and are a measure of capability. Instruments—useable power—are the potential of the capacity converted to capabilities. Effective power equals the appropriate instruments for the circumstances plus government effectiveness plus national will. *Effective power as other actors believe it to be is a signficant measure of state power.*[29]

The components of state power are interrelated and greater than the sum of the individual parts. Economic power results from the successful integration of natural resources with the capacity in terms of population, inclination, capability, and markets to generate wealth. It is derived from the integration of the other natural and social determinants of power. In turn, national wealth offers the opportunity to improve society, build and man strong militaries, and exert influence through effective diplomacy. State power is multifaceted and interrelated. Excessive expenditures on the military can deprive a society of an appropriate quality of life, while a heavy hand in diplomacy can create new adversaries and an indulged population may lack national will to use power. Political power is a measure of the appropriateness and effectiveness of government. What is its true nature—democratic or authoritarian? How well does it serve the needs of the nation—effectiveness and efficiency? And, how well is it supported—is there national will to act? Political power is closely related to the socio-psychological element of power and interdependent with the other elements. Socio-psychological power is reflective of national will and morale, national character, and cultural integration. From it a nation's determination and preferences for the application of power are derived. It may reside unequally in different parts of the population, and political elites may or may not represent its true nature. It has an impact on both the internal and external environments. Internally, it shapes the fabric of a state. Externally, it defines the state to others. An appealing socio-psychological profile may attract support and engender trust. It is in and of itself an informational tool of power. Information is an aspect of power that transcends all the social determinate elements. Military power has quantitative and qualitative components. Numbers of the best equipment count but leadership, morale, training, and discipline also have value. Capabilities, policy, strategy, and doctrine result in instruments that project this power. The relationship between diplomacy and military power is common knowledge, but the military element is also interrelated with the other social determinants.[30]

There are relationships among the elements and instruments of a state's power and the power of other states. A state's power is founded internally but in the international environment it is relative to the power of other states and contextual. For example, a state may have great reserves of oil, which if it is manged correctly can create economic power. Economic power can be parleyed into political power and military power. Yet, if a state lacks the character or will to develop and use this power in a particular situation, the political, military, and economic powers are not relevant. As Mahan argued in *The Influence of Seapower upon History* (1890), the nature of Great Britain's geography and population led to the creation of both seapower (economic power) and seaforce (military power) as instruments of power. The symbiotic relationship between seapower and seaforce created the British empire and along with effective diplomacy, another instrument, helped sustain and enhance it. The synergy of elements of powers converted effectively to the appropriate instruments in the context of the eighteenth and nineteenth centuries' international environment, when combined with national will and leadership, established a superior relationship for Great Britain among Great Powers that far exceeded the mere sumation of her elements.[31] Nonstate actors also possess some degree of power, and may exceed some states in particular aspects of the elements or instruments. Few have been able to combine all the elements as effectively and to the level of viable states.

Instruments of power are defined as the methods in which the resources derived from the elements of power of the state are applied. Instruments are how elements manifest themselves in strategy. Nuechterlein referred to these as instruments or tools of policy over twenty years ago in *America Overcommitted*. He lists and explains twenty instruments or tools. Under political and economic he lists eleven: diplomatic relations, scientific and cultural exchanges, humanitarian assistance, technical assistance, information and propaganda, economic and financial assistance, economic and trade policy, military assistance, covert actions, U.N. Security Council debate on a threat to peace, and trade embargo and economic sanctions. Under military instruments he lists another nine: military show of strength, expanded military surveillance, suspension/break in diplomatic relations, blockade/quarantine, partial mobilization and nuclear alert, localize use of tactical nuclear weapons, threatened use of strategic nuclear weapons, and limited use of strategic nuclear weapons. Obviously, he is writing in the Cold War, but his thinking is still instructive. The lists are also escalatory as presented, and he believed a higher intensity of an interest called for a higher level or stronger instrument. His view of a correlation of intensity of interest and the appropriate tool—one should neither over react nor under react—emphasized how instruments are used to signal state intentions.[32]

Some theorists and practitioners define the elements with greater specificity or in different terms, sometimes only identifying the associated instrument in a menu format as indicated in Figure 6.1. The informational element is a common substitute for the socio-pschological element of power. Sometimes these substitutions are only passing fads or leadership preferences and they can confuse or obsticate the extent of possible instruments inherent in the real element. For example, informational as a word has been so over used in the computer age that it is perhaps less helpful than the term socio-psychological it replaced in some paridigms. It is important to both understand the theory of power and to learn the operating paradigms of the various instruments. In the last ten years the Defense Department and some of the other interagency members have used several different models to highlight instructments of power: DIME (Diplomatic, Informational, Military, Economic), MIDLIFE (Militarty, Informational, Diplomatic, Legal, Intelligence, Finance, Economics), and DIMEFIL (adding Finance, Intelligence, and Law Enforcement to DIME).

Menus have their utility as aids as long as they do not limit the extent of the practitioner's thinking. Some instruments of power derived from the elements are obvious and longstanding, but instruments and combinations of the use of the instruments are really only limited by the resources available, the imagination of the strategist, the characteristics and vulnerabilities of other actors, and domestic and international acceptability.

Power is not absolute since it is contextual and relative to others. Contextually and relativity both limits and empowers strategy. Thomas C. Schelling in *Arms and Influence* (1966) addressed part of the nature of power. He argued that in the extreme power can be used to require compellence, make the adversary do something, or to create detterence, seek to prevent the adversary from doing something. Compellence has a positive aim. To be effective, compellence requires a deadline—comply by such a date or event or this action will be taken. Deterrence has a negative aim. Deterrence provides the adversary no deadline as its aims are indefinite—do not take this action. Deterrence is usually clear in regard to the undesired action and what will happen if it is taken. It has a degree of inherent stability because the assurance that if he does not act is credible—you are not punishing him now. Compellence is more problematic because it requires the adversary

Elements of National Power

TOOLS OF NATIONAL SECURITY POLICY

DIPLOMATIC	INFORMATION	MILITARY	ECONOMIC	FINANCE	INTELLIGENCE	LAW ENFORCEMENT
Diplomatic Recognition	Public Diplomacy	War	Trade Policy	Fiscal Policy	Knowledge	Review Decisions of National/Multinational Legal Organizations
Representation	Public Policy Statements	Nuclear Warfare	Trade Promotion	International Monetary Fund / World Bank	Analyzed Information	Treaty Compliance
Negotiation	Public Affairs/ Press Releases	Conventional Warfare	Trade Sanctions		Activity	
Advocacy	Diplomatic Demarches	Forcible Entry Strikes/Raids	Trade Alliances	Debt Forgiveness	Collection of Information	UN Security Council Resolutions
Signaling	Print, Electronic and Film	Unconventional Warfare	Economic Development	Taxes in Support of Elements of Power	Exchange of Intelligence Information with Other States/ Multinational Orgns	Customary International Law
Intimidation	Information Operations	Coercion/ Compellence/ Deterrence	Embargoes	Borrowing for Expenditures		
Coalition Building	Psychological Ops	Show of Force/ Freedom of Navigation Operations	Foreign Aid	Subsidy in Support of National Policy	External Training	Extradition
Consensus Building	Military Deception	Deploy Carrier Battle Group	Technology Controls	Freeze/Seize Monetary Assets	Covert/Paramilitary Activity	Stationing and Overflight Rights
Restrict Diplomatic Activities	Computer Network Operations	Blockade	Regulation	Monetary Policy		International Law Enforcement
Recall Ambassador	Electronic Warfare	Upgrade Alert Status	Environmental	Exchange Rates		
	Public Affairs	Overseas Presence				
Break Diplomatic Relations	Operations Security	Military Operations Other Than War/ Peace Support Operations				
		Arms Control				
Embassy Draw Down/NEO/Total Evacuation		Peace Enforcement/ Peacekeeping				
		Non-Combatant Evacuation Ops (NEO)				
		Humanitarian Assistance				
Coordination with International Organi- zations and NGOs		Scty Assistance/ Mil-Mil Contacts				
		Nation Building				
		Homeland Security				
		Military Assistance to Civil Authorities				

Figure 6.1 Elements and Instruments of Power.[33]

to act and, consequently, it begs questions about when, how fast, and how much is enough. Assurance is a much bigger issue with compellence, because the adversary must consider whether you will inflict additional punishment or raise your demands based on your success. Successful compellence and deterrence both require credible threats and assurances.[34]

While Schelling was focused on the bargining power in the use of force and nuclear weapons, his ideas in regard to a "vicious diplomacy" captured the essence of hard power whether it is military or economic. All power is about the ability to hurt according to Schelling. Understanding how to use hard power requires a distinction between brute force and coercion. Brute force is about taking what you want and is measured against the opponent's strength in the strategic calculation. It succeeds when it is used. It is not dependent on communications and signalling. A better army that takes and holds territory would be brute force. Coercive force is about the threat of pain if the adversary does not give you what you want. Therefore the threat has to be contingent on his behavior. Such power in theory is not relative, because it is not actually reduced by the opponent's ability to inflict pain. Yet the fear of consequences, the potentional infliction of some degree of pain on both sides, does make it relative. Consequently, it requires that interests not be absolutely opposed. Coercive power is applied through communications and signalling. The opponent must recognize that a threat is being made and be made to feel vulnerable. The understanding of the opponent, his culture, and his political and social fabric is essential to understanding when coercive power will work. Coercive power works best when it is held back, and the threat of its use creates the result. This attribute complicates the use of coercive power because if the threat is actually applied, the adversery often finds he can endure the pain, and the coercive effect of power gets weakened or lost. Air power theory and embargos rely heavily on coercive power. Understanding the difference between brute force and coercion is complicated because the same instruments and actions are used at different levels to take what you want or to signal. The difference often lies in the intent and is dependent on the adversary's understanding the intent as well.[35]

Power is more than brute force and coercion. Favorable outcomes can be achieved by inducement, offering a tangible economic or political benefit for a particular outcome. In a broad sense, it is fair to argue the United States is in a unipolar position in regard to military power. On the other hand, if the U.S. position is considered from an economic perspective, it is part of a multipolar structure that includes the European Union (EU), Japan, China, and others. Economic power is distributed and their general agreement is needed for favorable outcomes on international trade, antitrust, and financial regulations. The distribution of economic power creates interdependence that can work both ways. Power is even more widely distributed on other transnational issues such as terrorism, international crime, and climate change. Choices others make, even as small powers, can affect U.S.

interests. Inducements may be better than hard power in this environment. Others' behavior can also be influenced by attraction and co-opting of their motivations. If we understand others' preferences it is possible to get desirable outcomes without resorting to coercion or inducements. In other words, power is always relative and contextual.

What Joseph Nye refers to as soft power is such a strategic approach. Nye argues if other states admire a state's values, want to emulate its example, and aspire to its standard of living, it is possible to co-opt people rather than coerce them by getting them to willingly follow your agenda in world politics. Soft power is different from influence and persuasion—it attracts. Soft power is founded in the attractiveness of a state's culture, its political values, and its foreign policy. If they all are attractive, if the political values are lived up to at home and abroad, and if the foreign policy is perceived as legitimate and moral, the potential to exercise soft power exists. Soft power is not dependent on hard power, but it can work in collaboration with it. Soft power has limitations. It works better with similar cultures and is apt to be more general in its impact than producing a specific action or outcome. It also works better when political power is dispersed in the other state. Soft power has opportunity costs when it is misused or not used. It should not be imposed on an alien culture nor be perceived as being inconsistent in application. It creates opportunities and precludes issues when it is appropriate and consistent. Soft power is really about strategic choices that both reinforce and leverage what is good about a state. It motivates others to want the same outcomes through the attractiveness of the example.[36]

Good policy and strategy can make power more than the sum of its parts, but there are limits and constraints on power. Power is neither absolute nor unlimited. National policy and strategy that are founded primarily in one element or preference for a particular element of power is extremely limited in some applications. Strategic inflexibility can also be caused by single-mindedness or a lack of mental adroitness. Much like the game of "paper, scissors, rock," the state that enters the game with only one power or a known preference is subject to being more easily out played through the strategic choices of others. Power is also constrained or unleashed by domestic strategic culture and will. The international structure also poses practical, moral, and legal constraints. Other state power, individual or collective, is an obvious constraint on the use of power. While power itself is amoral—neither moral nor immoral, the choices in its use and in the perception of its use do have moral and legal implications. Theory also suggests there is a basis for moral and legal constraints. If a stable international order is founded on the twin pillars of an appropriate balance in the distribution of power and the sanctity of sovereignty as realist theory suggests, it begs the question of how should states interact other than through the coercive or direct application of power? Yet, state interaction in practice is about more than hard-power relationships.

Theorists wrestled with how states should interact long before West-phalia. Just War Theory is an attempt to constrain direct application of military power by establishing moral guidelines over decisions of whether to apply military power and decisions of how to apply military power. Just War Theory is readily available and is not revisited here, and quite frankly, when a state's vital or survival interests are at risk or nations are actually at war, its moral authority is less relevant. However, what is important to the national security professional is not where it has failed, but how often it has influenced strategic decisions and the effect it has in the international environment when it is obviously violated. Adherence to Just War gives a state a level of moral authority that attracts others to consider its case favorably and justifies the state's action, giving it a degree of legitimacy. Such power may be soft, but it has consequences. Moral authority and legitimacy apply to more than military power and are at the heart of idealism and institutional idealism, but neither are easy.

Legitimacy is inherently problematic for policy and strategy. As Edward C. Luck said: "Everyone wants to have it, but there is little agreement on where it comes from, what it looks like, or how more of it can be acquired."[37] Despite this confusion, there is agreement on two attributes of legitimacy. First, legitimacy is a subjective condition that is a product of perception, and second, that it really matters in the affairs of a state. In international politics, its conferment or denial along with confirmation or revocation are important because it makes the pursuit of interests easier or harder. It either smoothes the path or complicates it. For example, the U.S. invasion of Iraq had less legitimacy in the eyes of the world than the war in Afghanistan because it lacked specific United Nations approval, even though it was arguably the enforcement of an existing resolution. Consequently, finding allies and getting access to the capabilities of both IGOs and NGOs became more problematic, and the Arab street became more sympathetic to the terrorism that partially justified the invasion. It was further eroded when the primary justifications for intervention, WMD and support of terrorism, were discredited. Thus, the use of power achieves legitimacy when it is justifiable according to accepted rules, has evidence of consent, or appears morally justified. Legitimacy is always subjective and it can spontaneously emerge from a collective sense of fairness or be conferred by formal authorities or organizations.[38] It also has contextual and temporal components. The collective and world-wide public response and governmental support of U.S. action immediately following 9/11, which had both the spontaneous and formal conferring of legitimacy, are examples of the contextual and temporal attributes.

In a similar manner, the power of many international organizations, whether IGOs or NGOs, lies in their ability to provide services and the legitimacy that they enjoy or can confer on others. Hence, all legitimacy in the existing international order is about the appropriate exercise of power.

The rules of international order seek to provide peaceful, fair, and productive ways to pursue progress and changes in power relationships within the international environment. Large states seek legitimacy because it confirms their own moral justification for actions and strengthens their case in the eyes of the world. Small states tend to favor legitimacy as a way to constraint the power and autonomy of larger states. For states, legitimacy has both a domestic and international component—a need to appear to best serve the national interest and a need to be justified in the pursuit of any interest before the eyes of the world. Acquiring legitimacy rests in part in conformity to rules that have been negotiated or are a matter of practice in the international order, and in part to the expressed consent of all subordinate to the rules. Its value is also related to the concept of fairness, and an action confirmed by an IGO as legitimate that is perceived as unjust lessens the value of the conferred legitimacy. In the international political order, legitimacy is enforced by normative behavior, the idea that both individuals and the collective community will adhere to the rules. International law and organizations have a stronger attraction if they have a degree of universality and are perceived as furthering the interests and reflecting the values of a broad spectrum of states and peoples. Hence, to maintain their legitimacy the powerful must adhere to the agreed rules or norms of behavior and the lesser powers must not try to define the boundaries of legitimacy too narrowly or they risk the rules being routinely violated.[39]

In the struggle to exercise power favorably and reap the advantages of stability, states enter into various agreements. These agreements and other evolved practices in international politics place constraints or qualifications and obligations on the use of power. Such agreements and rules exist because they serve the collective interests of the states and the continuation of a stable international order. The power of such agreements and rules lies in their legitimacy, as discussed above, and in the will of the collective states to adhere to and enforce them. National security professions properly view these as both tools and constraints. The key questions are how do these affect interests, what should I do, what can I do, what must I account for, and what might others do in regard to these? In the strategic appraisal, the pertinent rules and agreements surface as strategic factors to be considered.

Both the schools of liberal institutionalism and constructivism view the evolution and combinations of international law, IGOs, international institutions, and accepted practices as transforming the modern international system into a constitutional order where international political organizations and legal institutions allocate rights and control the exercise of power by states. Some argue international law has evolved to a level where it competes with sovereignty as an organizing principal of international relations. International law is reflective of mankind's inherent search for order and security so that prosperity and progress can occur. In this view rule of law is seen as an independent basis of international order. International law and practices are well founded in history and constitute a body of laws and principles of action that govern relations among civilized states. The hierarchy among these is: (1) formal conventions, treaties, and agreements, such as the UN Charter or NATO; (2) customary international law, which are the accepted practices over time; (3) principles of law, which are leading ideas about municipal laws that should apply generally such as human rights; and (4) judicial decisions and the writings of jurists and scholars, such as the opinions of the International Court of Justice. Whether such a vision of a new international order is realized or not, clearly a post-modern process is ongoing and has resulted in a proliferation of laws, practices, and organizations and institutions that add complexity to policy and strategy formulation.[40]

The evolution to a post-modern international system is viewed differently by various constituents. The process has already created cracks in the geopolitical landscape between the United States and Europe. In the *Breaking of Nations* (2003) Robert Cooper argues persuasively that much of Europe's population has intellectually transitioned to a common view of shared interests, identity, and destiny. Inherent to their collective view is that an empowered global political order is the best way to manage power and maintain order. Without disputing the good intentions of such a goal, it is clear the European populations' perspective exaggerates the degree of order and legitimacy possible in the international environment and the ability of even an empowered IGO to act. Consequently, the perspective undermines their willingness to resource necessary state security instruments and limits participation in activities essential to maintaining an acceptable level of international stability to sustain globalization. It also often challenges the legitimacy of those state actors who do participate in sustaining order.[41] The strategist and national security professional must be aware of others' views of power and the implications for policy and strategy.

Legitimacy is also a consideration for many nonstate actors. Bureaucracies in IGOs, in order to retain their institutional power and relevance, must walk a thin line of impartiality in treatment of state actors. Many NGOs, as private organizations, seldom confer legitimacy on state actors because they see it as potentially compromising their reputations for impartiality, necessary for legitimacy, and often essential for freedom of access. However, NGOs are often quick to publicly question the motivations and legitimacy of state actors. NGOs' cooperation in particular situations is always a factor of their need for security and support and their views on impartiality and legitimacy. Policymakers and strategists must appreciate that legitimacy both empowers and limits choices and that both time and perception influence legitimacy's role. They must always appreciate that while legitimacy is partial to legal and moral righteousness, its favor can be sought, misdirected, and misused by others.

VUCA IN THE STRATEGIC ENVIRONMENT
AND MULTIORDERED EFFECTS

VUCA is inherent to the strategic environment. As articulated in strategic theory, this environment is a complex system of systems and is chaotic in its nature. In the international environment, VUCA is characteristic of both physical and humanistic systems. Weather, natural disasters, and equipment malfunctions—friction and chance—all illustrate the VUCA of physical systems. Yet, the level of VUCA in physical systems is relatively manageable in that it can be planned for and largely overcome or its strategic effects can be calculated and mitigated by simple strategy. Human systems introduce the greater VUCA in the international environment, and pose the greater challenge to strategic thinking. Friction and chance are also part of the humanistic systems, but the greater VUCA in humanistic systems is caused by human interaction. As Edward N, Luttwak so eloquently points out in *Strategy: The Logic of War and Peace* (rev. 2001), "only in the paradoxical realm of strategy would a choice arise at all" about whether to take the best and most direct course or seek advantage by taking a course that will fool your adversaries.[42] Luttwak is focused on war, where the advantage of surprise is most treasured, but as history reveals he could have been speaking about any strategy where the state's interests are at risk. States choose the road, easy or hard, that promises the best probability of success as they define it. They seek the most benefit in regard to power with a self-serving consideration of how it affects their sovereignty and their future opportunities in the international order. Making such choices is always complicated by a series of internal–external dialectics that convolutes direct cause and effect and complicates the calculation of advantage and risk.

Power and the pursuit of interests involve humanistic systems and judgments about other actors' motives and reactions. As a result, human attributes, such as resolve, willpower, intensity of preferences, emotions, values, culture, and intellect, contribute to and complicate any strategic calculation. For example, uncertainty about willingness to negotiate and trustworthiness on issues compounds the decision of how to use power, and states and actors often rely on "signaling" to convey their real intentions.[43] On the other hand, signaling intentions through power is often ambiguous and open to misinterpretation as Schelling points out. It can lead to greater uncertainty and volatility. Signaling may imply, or its success may create, unrealistic demands and set off an overreaction by the intended recipient. It may also create uncertainty about the stability of the existing order and cause reactions from other actors. Thus, three key humanistic components significantly contributing to VUCA in the international environment are intentions in regard to power, resolve, and trustworthiness. These components invariably cause multiordered effects that contribute to the security dilemma. VUCA is further compounded by chance and the numerous other relationships and interactions among the many complex systems constituting the strategic environment. Such relationships and interaction further contribute to the multiordered effects characteristic of complex and chaotic systems. Strategy introduces purposeful change into the environment to maintain the current status quo or create a new one. Neither can be accomplished without creating and, to some degree, favorably anticipating and using multiordered effects. Strategy does this through its selection of ends, ways, and means.

Understanding the role of multiordered effects and how to create and use them is inherent to successful policy and strategy. Effects can occur on multiple levels of causation in complex systems. First-order effects are direct cause and effect. Change is introduced and it has a direct (first order) effect on a part or parts of a complex system. Second-order effects are those changes that occur as a consequence of the first-order effects' interaction with each other and other parts of the complex system. Third-order effects are the effects that are created by the second-order effects and the interaction of the second-order effects with the results of the first-order effects, and the reaction of each individually and collectively with new parts and subsystems of the complex system or other complex systems. This ripple nature of effects continues in the environment—fourth order, fifth order, sixth order, etc.—until a new acceptable equilibrium is achieved. Such equilibrium (an acceptable level of stability) is achieved when the existing continuities and new changes are realigned within the system or some other effect has neutralized the impact of the original change and its multiordered effects. Anticipating the results of change is made even more difficult because randomness and chance play a role and, potentially, even all the first-order effects cannot be anticipated or even recognized as they occur. Hence, as effects ripple through the orders of magnitude, it is increasingly difficult to predict results—or from a theoretical perspective, you will get both predictable and unpredictable consequences within the complex systems constituting the strategic environment.

It is the VUCA in the strategic environment that complicates choosing the right strategy and accurately predicting results. To the degree the strategic environment as a whole can be assessed in the strategic appraisal process and to the degree the key strategic factors are identified and addressed by proper ends, ways, and means in strategy formulation, the more likely the desired multiordered effects will be created, and the more likely the desired end-state will be realized. The closer the multiordered effects approximate realization of the end-state; the more manageable any negative effects become. Creating and anticipating multiordered effects lie at the heart of strategy's success and merit more consideration than they have received previously in strategic theory.

Multiordered effects can be created and anticipated. Internal–external dialectics govern consideration of multiordered effects and guides the selection of ends, ways, and means in policy and strategy. The dialectic reflects the essential duality of the strategic environment as a complex system of systems. Strategic choices must always consider the internal system of which

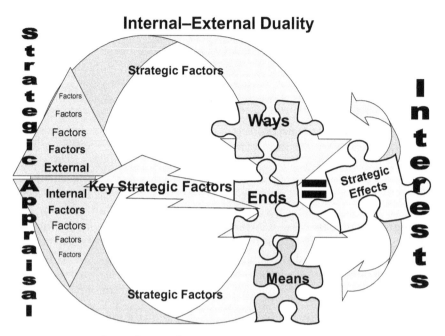

Figure 6.2 Interdependence of Factors, Strategy, and Effects.

the strategist is a part and the external systems that his changes will affect. Hence, the strategist in creating a strategy to be applied in the international environment is concerned with key questions focused on that aggregate external environment. What are the strategic factors that affect the national interest? Which of these factors must be addressed to protect the interest? Which of these factors can be addressed to advance the interest? How are the factors integrated into a synthesized and rational statement of ends, ways, and means? Can this strategy be executed and what are all the potential effects it can produce? Ultimately, do the collective effects support the desired end-state or detract from it? He is fundamentally considering issues of feasibility, acceptability, suitability, and risk in regard to his external environment. At the same time the strategist must consider questions in regard to his aggregate domestic environment. Will the resources be available? Is the national will there? Are the ends, ways, means, and effects acceptable to the leadership and the public? What are the potential unanticipated effects in the domestic environment? Will potential effects in international environment interact with the domestic environment? Are these interactions acceptable or will they affect the success of the strategy and the realization of the interest negatively? As depicted in Figure 6.2, the duality of internal–external relationships yield key strategic factors that provide the keys to ends, ways, and means that create positive effects for the interests.

This duality operates on multiple levels and affects consideration of all global, regional, state, or issue-focused strategies. It is at the root of multiordered effects and the security dilemma posed by any change within the strategic environment. In its simplest conceptualization, the strategist may be concerned with a policy issue involving another state and what his state should do about it. Since it is another state, its resolution lies in the international environment. Conceptually, the strategic issue is external and the state's decision is internal, or domestically determined. How the domestic environment functions in decision making is developed in detail in the following chapter, and here the intent is to only illustrate the nature of the dialectic. A strategist in the other state is conceptually in the same position. Theoretically, they could have compatible strategies that resulted in a bilateral peaceful resolution or conflictive strategies that were resolved bilaterally with force—a simple domestic–external duality exists conceptually for both in considering strategy. Multiordered effects need to be considered in regard to each domestic environment and the respective other state. However, issues in the international environment seldom lend themselves to this simple duality because they invariably involve other actors as a result of the nature of power and the need for an acceptable stability in the international order.

Hence, any single issue in the international environment potentially possesses complex internal–external dialectics. Following our state strategist and the policy-issue illustration, he must now also consider the rest of international environment in relation to the original two-state issue and whether and how they may choose to act—a new duality has been introduced. The domestic environment is now a given, and for a strategist always an iterative consideration in any strategy formulation. In the new dialectic as postulated here, other states may or may not have a direct or national interest in the particular policy issue, but all states will have a more or less general interest in the impact of its resolution on power distribution within the international order. Conceptually, all states with a direct interest in the issue and how it is resolved, including the two conflicting states, constitute the internal environment in regard to the issue and those without a direct interest constitute the external environment in regard to the issue. Now both strategists must be concerned with multiple internal and external environments, the dynamics of the issue among them, internal domestic dynamics of their own state, and the internal domestic dynamics of all the other actors or states and, further, their own state's internal dynamics in regard to the results of all resultant dynamics of all actors and states. If the strategy involves collective actors, such as alliances or coalitions, the complexity grows exponentially. An internal–external dialectic logically exists originally between the state and its alliance or coalition partners, and then again between that resolution and the other state, or opposing alliance or coalition. The dialectic is made more complex because all actors, not just states, must be considered. For a conceptual illustration of the dialectic see Figure 6.3.

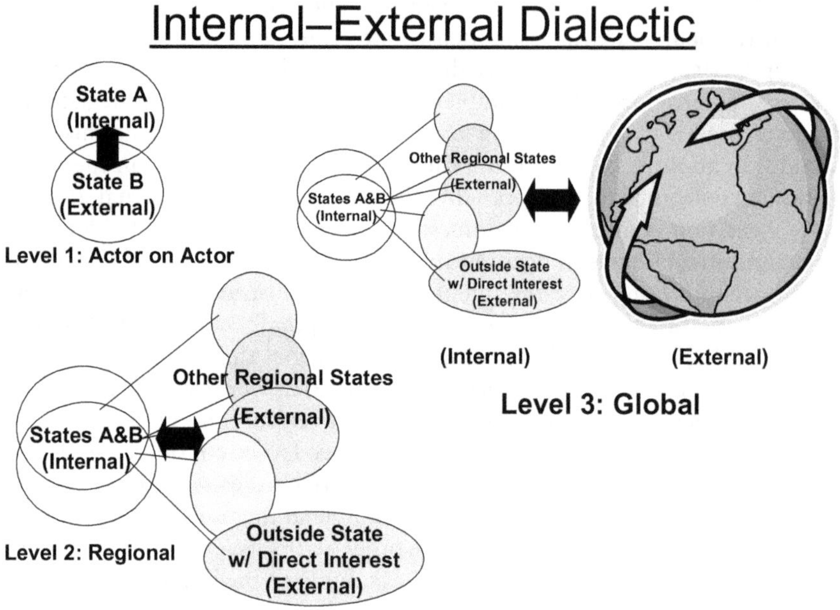

Internal–External Dialectic

Figure 6.3 The Creation of Multiordered Effects.

If the issue is regional, an even more complex dialectic exists in regard to the strategist's state and all the other states within the region. A second level of dialectic exists whereas the region is internal and the rest of the international environment is external. From an internal perspective the strategist is concerned with the first and second-order dynamics within his own state and other actors in the region. However, actors not internal to the region may perceive their interests or power relationships to be affected by the nature of the resolution. These actors will look at the issue and its potential resolution from their external perspective, calculating the internal dynamics and considering whether to act and how to act based on interests and their assessment of power. What these actors choose to do or not to do affects the internal decision-making dynamics of all other actors. In turn, the internal actors'—including our state strategist's—choices and actions potentially reactivate the internal and external dynamics of all. Every actor acts according to their own interests from their ideological and cultural perspectives in light of what they think is occurring or their assessment of the intent of others, and not necessarily according to actual facts or stated intentions. What each actor perceives as their best interest is a matter for the strategist to consider, and try to influence with his strategy. Complexity is increased when multiple issues are involved as internal and external multiordered effects occur on every level. In addition, chance and friction also play a role in these interactions. Hence, in addition to its physical systems with their own dynamics, the international and domestic strategic environments act as a complex human system of systems and the butterflies of chaos theory flutter here and there.

This condition might be considered hopeless except that power is not distributed evenly and is relative and contextual, and all actors pursue numerous and sometimes conflicting self-interests. A proper strategic appraisal can identify the states and other actors' real interests and separate what is really important in terms of factors from the overwhelming information flow and the limitless possibilities. Knowing what is really important—and focusing one's efforts on these key strategic factors—enables the strategist to identify objectives that usefully serve the interests and choose appropriate concepts and instruments of power to implement those objectives. It works because the strategic appraisal in identifying the strategic factors illuminates the interdependence and causal relationships among interests, strategic factors, relative and contextual power, and strategy.

How does this work in the real world? The U.S. invasion into Iraq provides an example of the dialectic and the dynamics. While the actual invasion began on March 20, 2003, led by the United States with a "coalition of the willing," the planning preceded the Bush administration and was reenergized in earnest following 9/11. With the advantage of hindsight, we can critique the strategic appraisal. We might legitimately question the validity of the process, or at least question the use of the appraisal in regard to strategy and planning. On the domestic side in the first level of the dialectic, two questions now standout. What should have domestic support for the war been based on and how long would the support last? On the first level in the international environment two key questions were what are Saddam Hussein's real intentions and what will really happen when he is deposed? On the second level, with the U.S. coalition and Iraq viewed as internal, the internal dialectic begged the questions of what will be the end-state in Iraq—the resolution of the conflict? And, what if that resolution falls short? On the second level, the external questions for the strategists were concerned with the other actors in the region. Questions should have surfaced in regard to the reactions of states, such as Iran, Turkey, Israel, Egypt, and Syria, and nonstate actors, such as Al Qaeda, Arab nationalist organizations, and the Islamic populations. Questions should have also arisen about French and Russian investments in Iraq: these investments made them regional actors. In the third level of the dialectic, internal questions would have asked how each of the possible outcomes in the region would affect the region and what regional actors might choose to do in regard to various plausible outcomes. It would also beg the question of the effect of each plausible outcome on the various U.S. interests in the region. External questions would be concerned with how the plausible outcomes would play in the rest of the international environment. Questions should have also arisen about how other state actors, IGOs, and NGOs might react to these potential outcomes. For example, Russia, China, and "old Europe" had clear concerns about the legitimacy and the near unilateral use of power inherent to the potential U.S. invasion. United Nations rhetoric at times reflected these nations' concerns, but it also reflected the collective concerns of many of the lesser nations along with those of the UN bureaucracy. By analyzing the potential scenarios on each of the levels from an internal–external dynamic, the astute policymaker or strategist may have concluded more time was appropriate, a case of a clear, unambiguous justification was needed at home and abroad, successful Phase-IV operations were the key to realizing the interest, or the change was not worth the blood and treasure required.

CONCLUSION

The international environment is that part of the strategic environment that is beyond the state's own domestic environment. It is the place where the state and all of its attributes interact with the rest of the world in hard- and soft-power relationships to advance or protect national interests. All of the actors in the international environment possess some degree of power. Power is not absolute; it is contextual and relative to others' power and interests. Hence, any state or actor can act proactively to create opportunities or leverage its power. The various actors in the international environment, and especially the states, are complex humanistic systems. The whole of the international environment—both its physical and nonphysical attributes— is a complex system of systems, consisting of both simple and complex systems. Interaction within and among these systems creates multiordered effects, resulting in VUCA and chaotic change. Both power relationships and interaction within the strategic environment can be understood to a great, but not complete, extent. Theories of international relations and a theory of strategy help to organize, interpret, and predict to some degree the reality of the international environment. They provide useful vocabulary and concepts for the strategic appraisal and strategy formulation processes. The strategist makes further use of these theories as he evaluates the internal– external dialectics of the strategic situation for his syntheses and evaluation of key strategic factors and determines how to affect them to create favorable multiordered effects. The favorable multiordered effects are created through his selection of ends, ways, and means for strategy.[44]

7

The Domestic Environment

...the ultimate source of strategy lies in the values of the people of a nation.[1]

—Henry E. Eccles

In this chapter the dynamics of the domestic environment are examined. National security professionals need to understand their domestic environment in order to formulate successful policy and strategy. The U.S. domestic environment is used as a model here, but the argument is that all states have a domestic or internal environment that interacts within itself to determine how the state will interact with the international environment. The domestic environment and international environment taken together constitute the strategic environment—and ultimately the holistic view is what is sought. As the duality of the internal–external dialectic suggests, strategy that does not explicitly consider the domestic environment interaction with the international environment will in the long run experience issues of acceptability and feasibility, even if initially these appear evident. Since the domestic environment is part of the strategic environment, the theory of strategy applies. In addition, while an IGO, NGO, MNC, or other actor organizations do not have the complexity of a state, the dynamics of internal interaction also apply to these and, if they are functioning on a strategic level, create similar issues. The strategist or policymaker then must concern himself with how the domestic environment affects what U.S. interests in the world are, how such interests must be articulated, the decision-making processes in regard to policy and strategy, and the formulation of ends, ways, and means that are suitable, feasible, and acceptable to both policymakers and the people.

THE PEOPLE, VALUES, AND NATIONAL WILL

In a democracy, the viability of policy and strategy is ultimately vested in the people. This is a fundamental fact with implications that policymakers and others often seem to fail to grasp. Policies and strategies that are not founded in the fundamental values of a nation's people risk not possessing, or over time losing, national will. Political will alone may sustain policy or strategy when there is no clash with important values, but ultimately political will must yield to the national will as expressed in the electoral process. The U.S. experience in Vietnam is a glaring example of this. Sustaining support for policy or strategy is made more difficult by the fact that national values often conflict and the relative importance can change over time as events unfold. For this reason, *both policy and strategy are domestically grounded in why something is undertaken as well as what is undertaken and how it is accomplished.*

National values vary in different societies based on culture and other considerations. National values are expressions of collective visions about what people believe represents a good life. They are an ideal statement of a desired and esteemed social reality: beliefs about idealized ways of living and acting. As such they serve as a means of determining and judging actual behavior based on beliefs about what society and its members should be achieving. Society's values when applied to specific issues or circumstances in the international environment help define national interests, the end-state desired. What is valued in one culture or society may be meaningless or objectionable in another. Not all values are of equal importance in any culture, and the importance of values can vary based on context or over time. Simplistically illustrated, good manners are not as important as individual liberty within the greater scheme of things in the United States, but good manners become relatively more important when the boss is coming to dinner tonight. Americans also value both national security and the worth of an individual's life.[2] When the American people believed Iraq posed a threat to national security, either as a result of weapons of mass destruction or affiliation with terrorists, they fully supported an invasion and the associated loss of American soldiers' lives. Americans also value democracy. However, the disassociation of the threats to national security and the Iraqi intransigence in forming a viable democracy have led many Americans over time to question the costs in soldiers' lives, reflecting their value of life. The national will for continuing the war and building a democratic Iraq has been affected over time by changes in context. To attempt to explain this change as political opportunism is to miss one of the fundamental ways national values play in policy and strategy's success. The national security professional is concerned with the values of other states because it gives him insights into their potential interests and strategic preferences. He is concerned with the values of his own state because they will determine interests and their relative intensity, and allow him to express interests with specificity so that their importance is clear to both decision makers and the general public.

The United States has a very large number of values. They are founded in the ancient Middle East and ancient Greece and Rome, but they are largely those western values shared by much of Europe with some peculiar American twists. They have been categorized in large subject areas, such as politics, law, religion, education, social values, science, economic, arts, and international relations, and listed in detail by some.[3] Others have taken a broader approach. Anita M. Arms, in an insightful and award winning article entitled "Strategic Culture: The American Mind" (1993), summarized the major historical influences forming American values as: the geography of isolationism, the ideology of individualism, education as an equalizer, religion as the rhetoric of moralism, and the effect of rapid change on the meaning of time and technology. As a result she states:

> ... the values that best describe American strategic culture are: the tendency toward isolationism; the adherence to an ideology based on individual rights and freedoms; the purely political interpretation of what it means to be American; the balance between the Protestant work ethic and capitalism; the moralistic approach to politics; the ethnocentrism born of the belief that Americans occupy the moral high ground; the chauvinistic opinion that the entire world aspires to be American; and the overwhelming need for immediate action and gratification.[4]

These values influence, and sometimes dictate, decisions and public support of political issues, international affairs, the value of negotiation, and the use of force—in other words, how America can choose to use her power.

America's unique national experience has created a peculiar set of values that differ from much of the rest of the world and is full of contradictions. Americans view government from a perspective of individual rights and responsiveness to an electorate. They believe in a special relationship between America and morality that makes it essential to define political issues in moral terms. This need often conflicts with America's basic pragmatism and results in confusing policy swings. America's rapid modernization and reliance on and success with technology make Americans somewhat impatient and sometimes overly concerned with quick, near-term results. Americans' value of human life makes them appear casualty averse by a reliance on technology to save collateral loss of life through precision—even as the lethality of individual weapon systems is increased. America is basically a peace loving country, and assumes peace is the natural condition. When Americans must fight they are normally compelled or motivated by ideals as opposed to an appeal to the realism of national security issues. Once committed, winning becomes everything. Americans are ambivalent in regard to world leadership. Americans vacillate from helping others and telling them what they should do to acting with total indifference while pursuing purely American self-interest. Some moralism is visible in every national security and foreign policy decision, because it justifies them in terms of our idealistic values. And last, but not least, even though our stated preference is for isolationism and nonmilitary solutions, once engaged we often seem to relish the recourse to war. These divergent beliefs and their manifestations represent contradictions that often make national will problematic and foreign policy and national security more difficult.[5]

"The people" is a useful term to use when discussing national consensus or national will, but it actually consists of different publics. A large segment of the U.S. population, some 75—80 percent, is a relatively uninformed public. In their day-to-day life, policy and strategy have little meaning, and they do not actively follow the issues of national security. One way national security gains meaning is when a policy or strategy has a direct impact on their life, such as a family member being in Iraq or gas prices rising dramatically. A second way is that extensive publicity can raise the concern with policy and strategy, such as when the news media bombarded the American people with charges of "genocide" in Bosnia. A third way is a conscientious communication effort by the government or others in support of or against a particular policy or strategy.[6]

A second segment, some 10—20 percent of the population, is considered informed public. Such people actively seek out information on national security issues through selective reading, regular news monitoring, and participation in discussion groups locally and on-line. This public often enjoys respect as a result of their relative success or position within their local community. However, they have little or no direct contact with the issues or governmental agencies and their understanding is based on secondary sources. While this group does not directly influence the agenda for national security issues, by virtue of their standing in the community they play a role in conveying information and shaping opinions in regard to national security decisions locally.[7]

A third group is the effective public. This elite group, some 5 percent of the population, is actively involved in influencing national security processes. They differ from the informed public because of their depth of knowledge and the centrality of foreign and defense matters to their personal and professional lives. They have roles as policymakers, actual members of government, and foreign policy experts. They may be found in elected office, academia, roles as national opinion leaders whose influence can actually affect policy agendas, think tanks, and various roles with special interest groups. And finally, a small group of core decision makers exists who are the actual people in government making the actual decisions in regard to policy and strategy. They occupy key positions in the executive and legislative branches, leading departments and agencies, or chairing key congressional committees. Formulating policy and strategy is done by the few in the name of the people, but national will resides in all the people. Building consensus and sustaining the national will for policy and strategy requires an understanding of the role and motivators of the different publics.[8]

There are competing visions for U.S. grand strategy as a result of disagreements on the overarching purpose of the United States and how it should interact with the rest of the world. Each competing vision has advocates who base their views on truth as they understand it based on their interpretation of U.S. values and historical experience and their observations and conclusions about the international environment. These competing visions have been broadly defined by the terms neo-isolationism, selective engagement, cooperative security, and primacy. They are presented here for contrast. An actual grand or national strategy uses aspects of all of them even though it may favor one over another.[9] For example, when the United States practiced "isolationism" in the early nineteenth century, it actively sought economic engagement around the world.

Neo-isolationism as a grand strategy advocates a minimal, necessary involvement with the rest of the world and heeds George Washington's advice to avoid entangling alliances. Such a view does not reject free trade, but would be leery of the modern mechanisms that enable globalization and entangle America into a web of commitments. It sees most of the world's problems as generated by disagreements among others, and therefore to be avoided as opposed to be solved by U.S. intervention. For neo-isolationists national interests are narrowly construed, diplomacy is limited, and military power is for defensive purposes only. Peace in their judgment is preserved by a judicious balance of power, but one in which the United States is a limited participant, if at all. It is a realist view, but one in which the United States flourishes by its noninvolvement in power disputes.[10] Of course, it assumes others will allow this noninvolvement and maintain a favorable balance in the international order.

Selective engagement is classical balance of power realism that acknowledges the primary issue in international relations is peace and security among the major powers. Consequently, advocates support the current order and seek ways to ensure stability by containing or intervening selectively in international crises and conflicts. Interests are restricted to those areas of the world that matter most to the United States. Economic and diplomatic full-time engagements are critical to this strategy's success, because they provide the primary instruments for intervention. Selective engagement requires the ability to project sufficient military forces to back up diplomatic positions and protect economic interests.[11] It is often problematic, because it appears to create a double standard as was the case in regard to intervention to prevent genocide in Eastern Europe as opposed to a policy of hands off in Africa.

Cooperative security is founded in the schools of liberalism and constructivism. At the core of this grand strategic outlook is the belief that peace is indivisible, and it is the obligation of all states to both work for it and enforce it. Interests are by their nature transnational and global security is an obligation. Such a strategy is prepared to intervene with the slightest provocation to ensure proper standards of state conduct. In the advocates' view, national economic interests cannot be separated from the global economy and the United States cannot go it alone. They believe effective diplomacy can resolve many issues. National sovereignty is not unimportant to this grand strategy, but must sometimes yield to the greater good. Military force is there to be used against transgressors, but will normally be integrated into a multilateral effort in order to ensure legitimacy.[12] Adherents to this view understand that it is difficult to get the necessary consensus to act in collective security arrangements, but believe the United Nation's organizational problems can be overcome with a proper structure.

Primacy is an extreme realist outlook that recognizes the maximum flexibility exists in the ability to act unilaterally. Its outlook is hegemonic, and its greatest security concern is the rise of a peer competitor. In this grand strategy outlook, interests are what the nation defines as interests and intervention occurs when and where the nation chooses to act to protect those interests. It focuses on economic and security interests. Diplomacy and economic power are important, but diplomacy is as prepared to "inform" as to negotiate. Military power supports and reinforces diplomacy and economic power, and acts as an enforcer. Consequently, this strategy must be supported by a military force structure that is unquestionably effective and capable of countering any single or collective of likely adversaries.[13]

The contradictions and paradoxes in American values and in U.S. strategic culture make interest definition and strategy formulation difficult. However, difficult or not, national interests are a reflection of prioritized national values in regard to an international situation expressed as a desired end-state. The strategist must understand national values and how they interact within the international environment, and among themselves, in order to articulate interests with sufficient clarity and specificity. Clarity and specificity ensure that policy makers can validate strategy in addressing the actual desired end-states and the American public can understand and support the need to realize the interests. In addition, the essentiality of sustained national will argues that strategy articulation must convey the "why" of its logic and purpose, as well as ends, ways, and means. The importance of articulating why is illustrated by the success of NSC 68: United States Programs and Objectives for National Security (April 14, 1950), or as it is perhaps better known—the Cold War Strategy of Containment.[14] Even though this document was not declassified until 1977, the logic of "why" in the strategy was so well made that it gave a unity of message to policymakers and politicians that carried conviction for the strategy for almost forty years, even if the specifics of implementation adapted to changing circumstances. NSC-68 pursued cooperative security and selective engagement. It rejected isolationism and primacy as too risky and too expensive.

THE BRANCHES OF GOVERNMENT

The policy of the United States in regard to foreign affairs and national security is formed and articulated by the elected government on behalf of the people. Consequently, all national strategies are products of the government. In a practical sense, most of the responsibility for policy articulation and strategy formulation resides with the president and the executive branch. However, the founding fathers were careful to preclude too powerful a chief executive by ensuring that certain formal authority for policy and strategy constitutionally resided in Congress. The judiciary also has authority in regard to U.S. law, and has on occasion ruled in regard to specific legislation affecting policy or strategy. In constructing the Constitution, the founding fathers clearly intended a degree of codetermination by the executive and legislative branches, with neither dominant nor subordinate in relation to the other.[15] This intent has made policy and strategy formulation, and its acceptance, more difficult since it potentially involves both in partisan politics. On the other hand, it has meant that major policy decisions generally enjoy political consensus at some point. Thus, the national security professional, even as a member of the executive branch of government, must be cognizant of congressional preferences and issues.

If constitutional checks and balances preclude a "ruling" presidency, the president nonetheless possesses immense advantages in setting the agenda in foreign affairs and national security. As the chief executive he presides over the federal bureaucracy, and all of the heads of the various departments and agencies respond and report to him. His advantage is strengthened to the degree his management style can focus this bureaucratic capacity—analytic capabilities, specialized knowledge, and subject-matter expertise—on his presidential goals as opposed to the pursuit of the various activities' own institutional interests. The growth in congressional staffers, the proliferation of special interest groups and think tanks, and internal competition among the executive agencies lessen this advantage, but are no substitute for it. The president is also the chief of state for the United States, a position that is separated from chief executive in many other democracies. As such, he is the symbolic representation of the state, and speaks internally and externally for the people. When well played, as with Ronald Regan, the bully pulpit creates and sustains national will. The president is also the commander in chief of the nation's military. More than a ceremonial expression of civilian control, this power has allowed presidents to conduct hostilities over 125 times without a declaration of war since the nation's founding. Other formal powers that relate to international relations and national security include: treaty negotiation; the nomination of key governmental personnel to office; the constitutional authority to recognize foreign governments; and, in practice, the power to commence or terminate diplomatic relations. While the Senate must consent in regard to treaties and appointment of key officials, such as military officers, diplomats, department secretaries, and judges, the presidential powers are significant and shape the direction of government. In some cases, executive power has been extended as is the case with executive agreements with other countries that do not require Senate approval, but bind the United States nonetheless.[16]

In addition to these formal powers, the president possesses a number of informal powers. Presidential singularity refers to the president's ability to speak and be recognized as a single voice of authority as the "leader" of the American people. No other single politician or legislative body can do this, nor command the respect and authority it conveys. By virtue of his office, the president also enjoys an inherent advantage in being able to shape public opinion. Success at taking advantage of this is dependent on his ability to use the media and personal popularity. Presidents also enjoy an advantage in international diplomacy. By using their personal credibility and leveraging techniques such as summits, they can create opportunities for changes abroad or at home. Presidential doctrines are another informal power. By unilaterally proclaiming doctrines bearing his name, a president can again shape foreign and national security policy by laying out a framework that defines the negotiation abroad and the debate at home. How well a president uses these powers depends on his own talent and leadership style, and on the recommendations and advice given to him. Each president establishes a decision-making management system that he thinks best serves him.[17] However, the national security professional should recognize the multiple possibilities for policy and strategy suggested by the formal and informal powers of the presidency.

Congressional powers for interacting with the international environment in foreign affairs and national security are also enumerated in the Constitution. They are specifically meant to act as a check and balance on executive power. Law-making authority resides in the two Houses of Congress. It gives Congress the power to create legal authority to take action or to forbid certain actions. The power allows Congress to adopt laws that define foreign and defense policy and grant or end additional authority of the presidency not defined in the Constitution. For example, the Helms-Burton Act in 1996 provided for U.S. citizens to sue foreign companies and citizens who traffic in Cuban property expropriated by Castro. This act essentially creates foreign policy because it extends U.S. jurisdiction to include events that occurred in a foreign country. This was done despite the objections of President William J. Clinton and his administration. On the other hand, Congress's agreement to fast tracking of trade agreements empowered the president by precluding congressional amendments and filibustering.[18]

Equally important, Congress has the power of oversight. Oversight power is inherent to the law-making power, and allows Congress to review the executive branch's implementation of a law. Some oversight is routine and non-problematic. However, if Congress has a special interest in a foreign policy or defense issue, this power can be employed quite dramatically as a public investigation. Congress is also the branch of government constitutionally empowered to declare war on behalf of the nation. While the president's role as commander in chief in committing forces to non-declared hostilities has appeared to make this power irrelevant, it has yet to be fully tested in court. The Constitution also gives Congress the power of the purse. This power gives Congress legislative control over what revenue can be raised, and how revenues can be spent. Since policy and strategy implementation are dependent on funding, the importance of congressional support is self-evident. The amount and nature of foreign aid, military force structure, training and education, organizations, and infrastructure—it all must be funded through Congress.[19]

Some constitutional powers are exclusive to the Senate. The Senate has confirmation power over those officials and officers nominated by the president and can reject nominations they find objectionable. Sometimes this power is used to force concessions from the president on other issues by refusing to act on nominations. The Senate also has the power of advice and consent in regard to treaties. Consent requires a two-thirds majority, making it difficult to commit the nation without consensus.[20] Historically, these two powers tend to make the Senate more engaged in international relations than the House, but in recent years the House has been more aggressive in using its fiscal and legislative roles to debate these issues in committee and on the floor.

Congress is a political institution that in many ways operates as it did at the founding of the nation. It is unique among modern legislative bodies in that it is a part of a separation of powers system. Gridlock is a natural and regular occurrence in a fragmented system where the executive and legislative branches have different national visions and political agendas.[21] Partisan politics, personal agendas, and organizational intrigue exist in Congress as well as the executive branch. In addition, congressional processes are antiquated, sometimes appear unfair and illogical, are often inefficient, and more often are slow. Attempts at improvements, such as more staff, have further slowed and complicated the political and administrative processes. Equally important, Congress has a dual nature. On the one hand, it is a collegial, institutional body seeking to make the best law for the land in accordance with the intent of the Constitution. On the other hand, it is made up of individuals whose electoral fortunes are based on their ability to represent and address the issues of their constituents. While the institutional role and individual role are interdependent, each places overwhelming demands on the congressman's time, requiring him to be both in Washington and back in his district. As one congressman insightfully pointed out in an office visit, it matters little what you think about national defense if you are not reelected to office. Congress operates by political imperatives, not by rules of good management.[22]

It does little good as a national security professional to be frustrated by political process. Congress is after all a political institution, and its purpose is to ensure reasonable consensus in the public interest—not maximize objectivity and efficiency. Individual power and self-worth in the body is founded in its complex committee structure, and it is unlikely to change.[23] On the other hand, no one in Congress is actively trying to keep the right policy and strategy from being approved and pursued—legislators want what is right for the nation, but there are legitimate differences among those responsible for policy. Consequently, both the debate and the resolution affect policy and strategy formulation and implementation. Policymakers and senior leaders are responsible for interfacing with Congress and engaging in the debate. However, many national security professionals at all levels interface with congressional staffers, advise senior leadership, and develop background material for use on Capitol Hill. From the professional's perspective, it is far more useful to understand how Congress works—both its statesmanship and shortcomings—and develop good policy and strategy that obviously serves the best interests of the nation and can be supported by all.

The judicial branch of government consists of the Supreme Court and the lower federal courts. The Supreme Court is part of the checks and balances of the Constitution and hears cases that challenge or seek interpretation of the Constitution or laws passed by Congress. While the strategist or national security professional of the past could think the judicial branch would be of little concern to them if they obeyed the law, this is increasingly less true in today's strategic environment. The proliferation and complexity of laws and treaties, the latter being laws once consented to by the Senate, and the overlapping of provisions and jurisdictions among laws, treaties, and executive agreements and directives create a morass that professionals can easily become bogged down in. A court can also broaden or extend an interpretation so that it nullifies key aspects of a strategy. For example, court rulings in regard to non-U.S. terrorist prisoners are forcing the rest of the government to rethink the whole issue of how to deal with such prisoners. Federal judges enjoy lifetime appointments and generally focus on their reading of the law and its intent, not the dictates of strategy or foreign policy and national defense.[24] In this environment, policy and strategy must have legal review.

THE EXECUTIVE AGENCIES AND THE INTERAGENCY PROCESS

Executive agencies is a term that is inclusive of the numerous cabinet-level secretaries and their departments, national councils, and other organizations comprising the federal bureaucracy that assists the president in meeting his constitutional obligations as both the chief executive and the head of state. It is through this bureaucracy that the president fulfills all his specified and assumed constitutional roles while he administers and enforces the laws passed by Congress. The bureaucracy is extensive and the intent here is not to describe it all but to highlight some key agencies and how the bureaucracy functions and makes decisions. In this regard, the professional must be keenly aware that in the modern world, with its global interconnectivity, context determines the relative importance among the agencies at a particular time and a holistic perspective is essential. Most important, in this strategic environment, the strategist and others must recognize the increasing criticality of the integration of capabilities and the value of a synthesized solution to most major issues.

Executive agencies are founded in law. Consequently, while in the hierarchal structure they are subordinate to the president, they are also subject to congressional oversight. Executive agencies are also subject to the power of the purse, and the consent of the Senate for the appointment of many of their officers. Structure within these agencies changes overtime, but a snapshot of today's bureaucracy is provided in Figure 7.1.

Various departments and agencies are organized differently and each tends to have its own organizational culture. That is, each has a set of organizational beliefs and assumptions that color what they perceive and how they think and feel about the issues. Organizational theory argues these manifest themselves in the way organizations behave, react, and interact externally, such as mission, goals, and control systems, and internally, such as language, norms of behavior, recognition, censure and status, and power relationships. Thus, each organization has its own values and norms and its own physical, behavioral, and verbal manifestations. It gets more complicated because large organizations have subcultures within them. For example, a simplified sketch of the U.S. army culture might identify loyalty as primary value, respect for rank as a norm, uniforms as a physical manifestation, saluting as a behavioral manifestation, and acronyms as a verbal manifestation. The army is actually a service subculture within the Department of Defense (DoD) and has internal subcultures organized around branches such as infantry, aviation, or logistics. At the same time the army is also a manifestation of what the greater American society wants in an army.[25]

Other services might share similar values, norms, and manifestations, but they would not be quite identical in these and what society expects of them is somewhat different. Congress saw service cultural differences as so significant to military effectiveness that they passed specific legislation

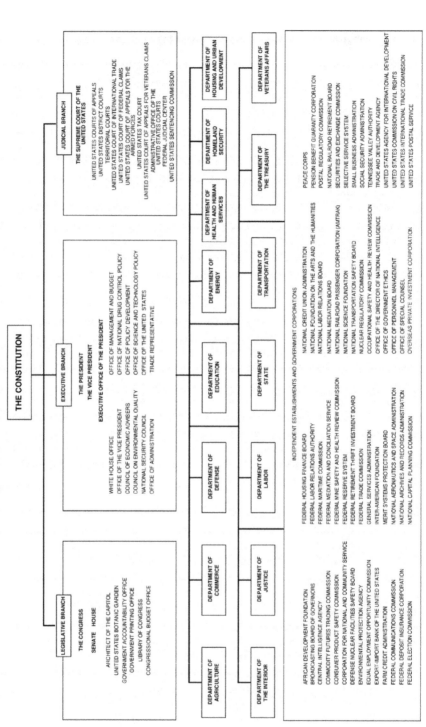

Figure 7.1 The U.S. Government Bureaucracy.[26]

affecting assignments, promotions, and education to ensure the military officer corps could work together in joint warfare. Civil employees in the DoD differ somewhat in culture from any of the services for similar reasons. You can observe the impact of culture play out when new political appointees arrive at DoD or in the Service offices. They have to learn how to fit in the government civilian culture while learning how to interact with the different service cultures. Differences are even more evident and further complicate interaction when it is between agencies. For example, when a uniformed service member must interact with a State Department official or employee differing cultural perspectives of time, authority, and resources often lead to misunderstanding. Strategists and national security professionals must recognize these differences and take advantage of the positive attributes of organizational culture and work around the downsides in order to craft effective policy and strategy. Cultures contribute to the VUCA (volatility, uncertainty, complexity, and ambiguity) of the domestic environment, but cultural diversity informs creativity and broadens policy and strategy options.

Other dynamics are at work within the departments and agencies and within organizations and among organizations when they must work together in a common effort. It should be obvious that personalities matter and that the importance of personality is context dependent. Many thought that Secretary of Defense Donald Rumsfeld's tenure as secretary was in question before 9/11 as a result of the controversy his leadership style and his vision for DoD caused among the services. Immediately after 9/11, the same forcefulness, bluntness, and single-mindedness were characterized as strengths, only to resurface later as issues with his leadership.[27] Individual ambition and organizational pride and prestige are other factors that affect collaborative efforts. The negative consequences of dysfunctional personal ambition are fairly well understood. Organizational pride and prestige can also lead to dysfunctional efforts. Depending on the issue, who guides the decision and who gets the credit can be disruptive. Sometimes there is a degree of competition and jealousy among the departments and agencies, and among the principals representing them, which infects the whole collaborative process of government. Classically, the State Department and the DoD are interdependent with military power giving substance to diplomacy and diplomacy parleying military force into political success. Yet, each is overly protective of what they perceive as their turf, and disruptive disputes have existed between the secretaries and the organizations. Secretary Rumsfeld and Secretary of State Colin Powell's disagreement over the necessity of gaining the legitimacy of United Nations approval for invading Iraq and the potential problems of a post-war Iraq could well have been genuine policy disagreements, but who is at fault for the current failure to bring stability—a military failure or State's intransigence—remains a sore point between and within the two departments.[28]

Historically, the decision-making framework in the executive branch has followed one of the three general patterns characterized as competitive decision making, collegial, and formalistic. The type of framework is determined by the president and his preferences for a management style. The term framework applies to how the president chooses to get his information and recommendations, not to how the decision is actually made. Franklin Roosevelt used a competitive decision-making framework in which he deliberately encouraged competition and conflict among his cabinet heads so that important decisions made it to his desk. He sought access to all points of view and the maximum input. It fitted his personality and somewhat unique abilities, but has not been the primary style of any other president. Some theorists believe the VUCA of the current strategic environment is too daunting to make this model viable. The collegial framework relies on a close-knit team that is comfortable with one another. While the president remains the first among equals, this model encourages a free and open exchange of ideas among the team. John Kennedy used this model as it appeared to fit his personality, need to be involved with details, and personal expertise. Under optimal conditions this style works well, but was problematic as a framework in the Jimmy Carter administration where a coherent vision and foreign policy expertise appeared to be lacking. The collegial style tends to exclude outside perspectives and can be somewhat myopic in regard to the overall picture of foreign policy and national defense.[29]

The VUCA of the modern strategic environment has increasingly driven presidents to a formalistic framework. This model relies on a formal structure that is designed to ensure key decisions and essential information are forward upward to the president, while lesser issues are resolved within the bureaucracy by decisions made at lower levels. Its value has been validated by its reliability in creating successful policy options. Today, the formalistic framework is commonly referred to as the interagency process. And while presidents have used slightly different organizations and renamed and revamped the processes to fit their style and preferences, it has remained essentially the same.[30]

A formal mechanism, known as the National Security Council (NSC), for providing national security advice to the president is required by the National Security Act of 1947, as amended and clarified in 1949. It is a part of the executive office of the president. Congress mandated the NSC to ensure that presidential decision making was informed by the appropriate executive department officials, particularly in regard to national defense policy. National security was considered to be focused in three broad areas: the defense of the United States, protection of our constitutional system of government, and advancement of U.S. interests around the world. Presidents have interpreted these broadly to include domestic, foreign, military, intelligence, and economic policy affecting national security. The law provides for

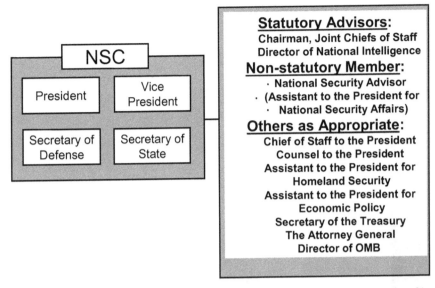

Statutory Advisors:
Chairman, Joint Chiefs of Staff
Director of National Intelligence

Non-statutory Member:
· National Security Advisor
· (Assistant to the President for
· National Security Affairs)

Others as Appropriate:
Chief of Staff to the President
Counsel to the President
Assistant to the President for
Homeland Security
Assistant to the President for
Economic Policy
Secretary of the Treasury
The Attorney General
Director of OMB

NSC

President | Vice President

Secretary of Defense | Secretary of State

Figure 7.2 Organization and Members of the National Security Council.[31]

statutory and non-statutory members. The NSC is chaired by the president. Statutory members include the president, the vice president, the secretary of state, and the secretary of Defense. The statue also legitimizes advisory roles for the director of the National Intelligence Agency and the chairman of the joint chiefs of staff. The directors of the Arms Control and Disarmament Agency and the United States Information Agency are special advisors. The president can appoint additional members or invite anyone else he desires to regular meetings. Who these may be has varied over time, but usually includes the assistant to the president for national security affairs, the chief of staff to the President, the counsel to the president, and the assistant to the president for economic policy. Other heads of executive departments and agencies attend as appropriate when issues concerning their agencies are discussed. An illustration of membership is depicted in Figure 7.2. Presidents have used the NSC to varying degrees, but the trend has been for its role and its various supporting staffs to increase.[32]

The NSC and its supporting structures are designed to elevate the information and decisions that ultimately need to be made at the White House level. The NSC also serves as the means for coordinating policies across agencies. In order to do this an NSC staff exists and a number of standing committees have been created. The organization of the NSC staff and the number, kinds, and purposes of committees are determined by the president, usually as one of his first actions in office. The assistant to the president for

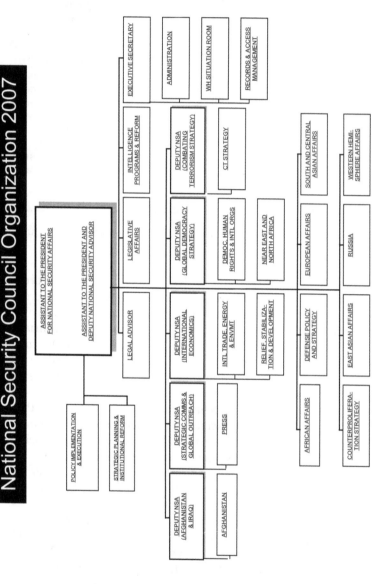

National Security Council Organization 2007

ASSISTANT TO THE PRESIDENT FOR NATIONAL SECURITY AFFAIRS

ASSISTANT TO THE PRESIDENT AND DEPUTY NATIONAL SECURITY ADVISOR

- POLICY IMPLEMENTATION & EXECUTION
- STRATEGIC PLANNING & INSTITUTIONAL REFORM

DEPUTY NSA (AFGHANISTAN & IRAQ)
- AFGHANISTAN

DEPUTY NSA (STRATEGIC COMMS & GLOBAL OUTREACH)
- PRESS

EXECUTIVE SECRETARY
- ADMINISTRATION
- WH SITUATION ROOM
- RECORDS & ACCESS MANAGEMENT

INTELLIGENCE PROGRAMS & REFORM

LEGISLATIVE AFFAIRS

LEGAL ADVISOR

DEPUTY NSA (COMBATING TERRORISM STRATEGY)
- CT STRATEGY

DEPUTY NSA (GLOBAL DEMOCRACY STRATEGY)
- DEMOC, HUMAN RIGHTS & INTL ORGS
- NEAR EAST AND NORTH AFRICA

DEPUTY NSA (INTERNATIONAL ECONOMICS)
- INTL TRADE, ENERGY & ENVMT
- RELIEF, STABILIZA-TION & DEVELOPMENT

- SOUTH AND CENTRAL ASIAN AFFAIRS
- WESTERN HEMI-SPHERE AFFAIRS

- EUROPEAN AFFAIRS
- RUSSIA

- DEFENSE POLICY AND STRATEGY
- EAST ASIAN AFFAIRS

- AFRICAN AFFAIRS
- COUNTERPROLIFERA-TION STRATEGY

Figure 7.3 Bush Administration NSC Staff.[33]

national security affairs (national security advisor) and members of the NSC staff are part of the executive office and fall under executive privilege in their interface with Congress.

The national security advisor and an NSC staff assist the president in national security and foreign policy issues. The staff is headed by an executive secretary, but receives its direction from the president through the national security advisor. This staff serves a variety of functions for the president to include: provide information and policy advice, manage the interagency policy coordination process, monitor implementation of policy decisions, oversee crisis management, provide support for negotiations, articulate policies in media, conduct preparation for meetings with foreign leaders and foreign travel, prepare presidential briefings, response to congressional inquiries, and prepare public remarks for the president. It also serves as the initial point of contact for agencies wanting to bring a policy issue to the president's attention. The NSC staff organization changes over time. For example, in the Clinton administration, it was organized geographically, functionally, and as support offices: executive secretariat; administrative office; African affairs, Asian affairs, defense policy and arms control, environmental affairs, European affairs, foreign policy speechwriting, intelligence programs, international economic affairs, international health affairs, inter-American affairs, legal affairs, legislative affairs, multilateral and humanitarian affairs, near east and south Asian affairs, nonproliferation and export controls, press, records and access management, Russia/Ukraine/Eurasian affairs, southeast European affairs, systems and technical planning, transnational threats, and White House situation room.[34] Despite periodic cutbacks to rein in its growth, the complexity of policy has pushed toward larger NSC staffs. President Bush's NSC staff in 2007, depicted in Figure 7.3, has grown from what he originally intended. Often increases are achieved by detailing from the departments and agencies of the executive branch to give the appearance of no growth. This practice brings new perspectives on to the staff, but also creates some issues with the departments and agencies.

The membership of the NSC, beyond the statutory members, and the establishment of the current committees depicted in Figure 7.4 was directed by President Bush in National Security Presidential Directive 1 (NSPD-1), February 13, 2001. It is informative to note that President Bush directed that NSPDs replace both Presidential Decision Directives (PDDs) and Presidential Review Directives (PRDs) as instruments to communicate presidential decisions on national security policies. Thus, like his predecessors before him, he put a personal touch on the NSC mechanisms to make them distinct. In the same document he also made changes to the committee organizational structure. He retained the NSC principals committee from the Clinton administration and designated its specific membership. It remains the senior interagency forum for consideration of policy issues affecting national security. The principals committee is essentially the NSC without the president

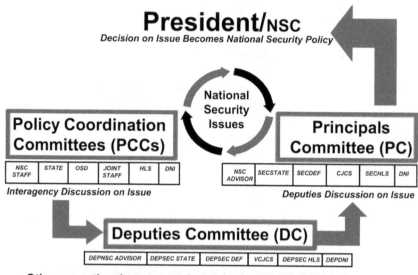

Figure 7.4 Bush Administration Interagency Process.[35]

and includes others as indicated below. It meets at the call of the assistant to the president for national security affairs. NSPD-1 specifies that specific individuals will be included if issues in their area of responsibility are to be discussed, thus legitimizing their right to be present. He also retained the NSC Deputies Committee (DC), which is the senior sub-cabinet level interagency forum for consideration of policy issues. It is empowered to ensure that issues have been properly analyzed and prepared for decisions. As part of the empowerment this committee can prescribe and review the work of subordinate interagency working groups. Any member of the DC may request a meeting to facilitate prompt resolution of a crisis. NSPD-1 also noted that the president or vice president may attend any and all meetings.[36]

The day-to-day management of the development, coordination, and implementation of national security policies is accomplished in the Bush administration by the national security council policy coordination committees. These committees are formed from members of the various departments and agencies represented in the DC and provide policy analysis and recommendations for consideration by the more senior committees of the NSC committee system. They also ensure decisions made by the president are implemented in a timely manner. NSPD-1 established six regional Policy Coordination Committees (PCCs) chaired by under secretaries or assistant secretaries designated by the secretary of state. It also established eleven functional PCCs designating varying authorities appointing chairs of like

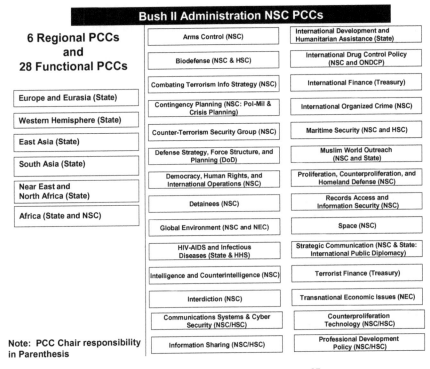

Figure 7.5 Policy Coordination Council Organization.[37]

statute as the regional PCC chairs. By 2007 the number of functional PCCs had grown to twenty-eight. Each of the PCCs has an executive secretary appointed from the NSC staff by the national security advisor to ensure the NSC staff is informed and to assist in regard to scheduling, agenda setting, and record keeping. Chairpersons of the PCCs may invite attendance from non-member agencies with approval of the executive secretary of the NSC staff. Interagency Working Groups (IWGs), the committees at this level in the previous administration were abolished, as were all other interagency ad hoc groups of any type except for those provided for in legislation. Provisions were made in NSPD-1 for the reestablishment of some of these groups as subordinate working groups, if justified.[38] The current PCC structure, titles, and chair responsibility are depicted in Figure 7.5.

In NSPD-1, President Bush sought to establish a formal, hierarchical structure that he believed was consistent with his management style as the chief executive and his philosophy of smaller government. Stating that he wanted to further clarify responsibilities and create effective accountability, he also eliminated existing special presidential emissaries, special envoys for the president, senior advisors to the president and the secretary of state, and special advisors to the president and the secretary of state, unless specifically re-designated or reestablished by the secretary of state as positions in that department.[39] The need to clean house with a new political party in the White House notwithstanding, in this regard he followed an established pattern set by his predecessors, and one that, if the past is any indicator, future presidents are also likely to follow. In his changes, he streamlined the structure initially, but conforming to past experience it has subsequently grown as a result of the numerous and complex national security issues confronting the United States. It is also important to note that the restructuring did not solve any of the organizational bias, departmental and agency rivalries, or institutional conflicts with Congress that challenged policymaking in the past. Such issues are part of the VUCA of the domestic environment.

Other concerns about the interagency process also exist. Often presidents have had the formal structure, but have tended to centralize decision making at the top based on heuristics independent of the formal structure and creating a top down-driven system. The problem associated with this practice is that the actual knowledge resides at the lower levels, and such a top-down system denies the leadership both information and options. For example, one common explanation of the failure to be prepared for the post-conflict operations in Iraq is that the secretary of Defense and the vice president precluded key information about potential issues from reaching President Bush's ears by not allowing the entire interagency system to work as it was designed. Whether the need for secrecy or a deliberate exclusion precluded full interagency input, it is clear that many of the post-conflict problems were commonly known among the lower echelons of the interagency system.[40] Another problem is that when the president relies on only a few trusted advisors, the potential for groupthink exists. A president's trust in these advisors is often founded in their like-mindedness in regard to political ideology and worldview. Consequently, the president often hears what he already knows and believes, not the full range of potential policy options that should surface through a system where career personnel are protected by civil service or other guarantees.[41]

In some previous administrations the focus on national security in the interagency process was not comprehensive. Prior to President Clinton, there was no formal economic perspective in the NSC interagency process. This has been remedied by including the Assistant to the President for Economic Policy in the NSC and other representation when specific economic issues are addressed. It has even been increased by the addition of a separate National Economic Council, which coordinates the economic policymaking process with respect to domestic and international economic issues. This office ensures that economic policy decisions and programs are consistent with the president's stated goals and ensures those goals are effectively pursued.[42] A Homeland Security Council system has also been established to help inform the president on homeland security issues specifically.[43] These structures are also part of the interagency process and in theory work similar to the NSC procedures discussed above. In practice, the value and power of all such councils are rooted in their utility and influence in presidential decision making. For example, the Washington reality is that partisan political considerations always pervade the creation of this level of council. The real purpose of establishing and sustaining such councils may be to either legitimately respond to real needs or deflect attention away from administration failures, or some combination of the two. While coordination among the agencies is always helpful, it remains to be seen if any council in a particular administration adds value to the decision-making process or simply confuses and delays it.

Interagency work at any level is difficult. First, it is a process and not an organization. Lines of authority are not clear and most participants are representatives of their particular department or agency, and each has vested interests. Personnel turnover in the PCC structure is common, and it takes time to build working relationships and trust. Specific subject matter expertise in regard to particular issues can often be lacking in the appointed committee members at all levels and technical expertise must often be brought in, slowing the analysis and recommendation processes. And fundamentally, the interagency process is a bureaucratic process that represents the various government bureaucracies with all the advantages and disadvantages of bureaucracies—the latter being compounded by cultural and equity differences. The differences between military and civilian cultures are obvious, but each department has its own organizational culture that can inhibit the interagency process even as it brings diversity to the deliberations. Misunderstandings in regard to differences in roles, missions, and capabilities can also add to the confusion, as do differing procedures and security considerations. Rivalries and tensions within and among the various agencies exist in regard to power, and resources are always an issue. Coordination is in part a ceding of control: bureaucracies do not easily do this. Real questions as to the role and value of the interagency process exist, but the coordination of policy and strategy is essential. Hence, whether considering the process or the product, there is value in this structure.

An interagency process also exists outside of the Washington, D.C. area. Each ambassador has a country team that is composed of members of the various departments and agencies assigned to the embassy or working in the host country. The country team advises the ambassador and under his supervision coordinates all of the various U.S. government activities within the host country. The importance of effective interagency coordination on the success of policy and strategy has not been lost on the military either. Combatant commanders, through the cooperation of the other departments and agencies, have built up interagency teams that provide advice on regional strategy and assist in planning. Success has led to procedures for prototyping joint interagency coordination groups that provide for a more formal interagency process at the theater and operational levels. The nature of the issues confronting the United States in some regions makes the idea of an integrated military and civilian combatant command very appealing. The new combatant command, Africa Command, announced by President Bush in February of 2007 will have an integrated leadership and staff with a military commander and an ambassador from the State Department serving as a deputy, hopefully institutionalizing a successful interagency approach.[44]

A big issue in the formalistic approach just described is whether this structure, and in particular the national security advisor, functions as a policy facilitator, a policymaker, an honest broker, or a policy advocate? Presidents, national security advisors, and Congress have differed over this based on the incumbent president's style, the residing national security advisor's capabilities and personality, and the issues of the day. Congress continues to keep a watchful eye on the interagency process and many legislators believe the system needs to be reformed in order to bring it under greater congressional scrutiny. The system can be exclusionary and duplicitous. Examples, such as the Iran-Contra Affair during the Regan Administration, indicate the potential for errors in judgment and illegal actions when the NSC staff becomes too empowered and proactive. Some think tanks are now advocating a stronger role for the interagency process by permanently sitting staff members and giving more authority to permanent committees at the expense of department and activity heads. They talk in terms of the interagency arena as outside and distinct from normal department or agency responsibilities, perhaps reporting more directly to the president through the national security advisor and having control of funding for the issues they work.[45] Questions about the precise nature and roles of the NSC and other councils will continue to confront future administrations and the Congress, but the answers are not clear. What is clear is that both the international and domestic environments are increasingly VUCA and the United States needs both informed and active statesmen along with a mechanism that allows these statesmen to understand how to use the immense power of the United States to best advantage.

OTHER INFLUENCES ON POLICY AND STRATEGY

In the domestic environment there are a wide range of influencers affecting policy and strategy formulation and a national consensus in regard to them. These influencers can be usefully categorized as think tanks, academia, special interest groups, and the formal and informal media; however, these distinctions are often blurred in practice. Understanding these nongovernmental influencers is important because they actively seek to inform or influence the public's, the politicians', and the policymakers' judgment in regard to the nation's purpose and its policy and strategy. Nor are any in the national security community free from this influence. In fact, some of the influencers are a part of the community and many of the influencers play a productive and essential role in national security and public life in a democracy. The national security profession must understand who are these influencers and the parts they play in regard to information, policy, public opinion, building a national consensus, and sustaining national will.

In a pure sense think tanks are nonpartisan, not-for-profit, research institutions established to study and proposed viable and appropriate public policy. They are staffed by individuals with specific expertise in a wide range of international and domestic policy areas—national security, foreign affairs, economics, international relations, political science, trade, etc. They bridge the gap between policymakers and the various publics, often serving a vital public role in providing detailed research and thoughtful policy alternatives to both the legislative and executive branches.[46] Examples of think tanks include the Carnegie Endowment for International Peace, the Center for Strategic and International Studies, the Brookings Institute, the CATO Institute, Rand Corporation, and the Hoover Institution. Many of the think tanks are located in the Washington, D.C. area, but others are in the larger metropolitan areas on both the east and west coast. A number of think tanks are part of, or associated with, and collocated with major educational institutions. In addition, each of the nation's War Colleges has a research-focused component that analyzes and evaluates policy and strategy, such as the Strategic Studies Institute at the U.S. Army War College. Think tanks are not unique to the United States and foreign think tanks offer insights into international thinking and fresh perspectives to both national and global issues.

Think tanks were originally characterized by their nonpartisanship, scholarly approach, and the people who work for them. Academicians, retired military and other national security professionals, and some former policymakers favor employment at these places because of their objectivity and nonpartisan approach to issues. While some think tanks clearly have ideological preferences, they strive hard to maintain a reputation for objectivity and quality in research.[47] As a result, their research work is useful for the policymaker and strategist, decision makers, or other members of the effective public. Such institutions' products contribute to the holistic perspective required of strategic thinking at any level. A strategic thinker should cultivate a group of diverse and reliable sources among these institutional experts, much like the stock buyer seeks to build a diversified and balance portfolio.

Academicians working within educational institutions also provide opportunities for the national security professional to research issues and broaden his perspective. The "publish or perish" mentality characteristic of many universities, and the academic's inherent desire to share knowledge, create an annual deluge of books and articles relevant to national security. Within this hodgepodge the national security professional can find applicable theory, useful case studies, and detailed and nuanced studies of states, cultures, and policy and strategy. One advantage of academic literature is that it is invariably peer reviewed prior to publication, or shortly thereafter. Peer review enhances and assesses value and reliability, often providing alternative viewpoints. The national security professional should be immersed in this scholarship.

Interest groups are organized groups of people who actively seek to influence public policy in the direction of their particular interest or interests. They are organizations of like-minded people with a political agenda. Such groups serve a useful public purpose in that they attempt to consolidate the concerns of people and represent those concerns in the political process. It is a form of modern pluralism and enshrined in the Constitution under the right to petition the government. Many interest groups share much in common with think tanks, and the information and perspective they seek to share are useful. However, interest groups are established to advance particular interests or ideologies and their activities are reflective of that.[48]

Generally, interest-group activities can be categorized as lobbying, education, and pressure. Many participate in all three, and the titles are sufficiently descriptive that little further explanation is required. Such groups may be private or public, permanent or ad hoc, national or international, and general or specific. While most of interest-group activities are above board and serve a useful function, their primary purpose is to advance their specific viewpoint and they are often partisan in outlook. They can, in fact, represent the interests of other governments or foreign businesses. They can also represent those opposed to the use of necessary and essential instruments of power, such as the military or coercive diplomacy. Like think tanks, interest groups get their funding from various sources, and the funding trail is often illustrative. Depending on their emphasis in activities, interest groups attract a variety of employees, but often tend to have more politicians than experienced professionals on their staffs. Interest groups often create foundations and research institutions to enhance their prestige and credibility.[49] While they add to the diversity of perspective, the national security professional must assess the reliability and understand the potential bias of interest-group resources.

Some private volunteer organizations and domestic and international NGOs also play roles in influencing policy decisions and strategy that are not quite the same as the traditional interest group. Church and civic organizations mainly have a local focus but can be mobilized or self mobilize on policy issues. For example, apartheid in South Africa created spontaneous political activism among church groups. Amnesty International and the International Red Cross have the ability to create headlines and lead stories affecting the legitimacy and morality of U.S. actions or influence large segments of the population to demand action by the U.S. government on international atrocities and incidents. Publicity around these organizations' issues can influence policy, but their influence is often transient or aimed at a global audience.

The biggest influencer is the media for it is the megaphone of many and a voice of its own. Sometimes referred to as the fourth estate to suggest its role and influence on U.S. politics, the printed press, early radio, and television have historically played a role as democracy's watchdog in regard to policymaking and strategy. By the middle of the twentieth century the old media had arguably begun to define itself as a profession with standards for reporting and commentary that materially enhanced the national debate on policy and strategy. In this debate, the media and the government enjoyed mutually supporting agendas. The government needed to get official and correct information out to the American people, and the news media needed government "news" to fulfill their idealized professional role of monitoring the government and keeping the American public informed. Even though both often fell short of these high aspirations, the relationship was fundamentally sound. The power of the news media over policy and strategy was significant, but related to the role of democracy's watchdog and guided by self-enforcement of professional standards for objectivity and balance. As such, the media represented a valuable two-way channel and an essential confirmation of communication between the people and their government. For example, contrary to a somewhat popular belief that President Lyndon Baines Johnson (LBJ) attributed the loss of the Vietnam War to Walter Cronkite's editorial comments in February of 1968, President Johnson was simply acknowledging that the watchdog had barked. "For it seems now more certain than ever," Cronkite said on his broadcast on CBS Evening News, "that the bloody experience of Vietnam is to end in a stalemate." After watching Cronkite's broadcast, LBJ was quoted as saying. "That's it. If I've lost Cronkite, I've lost middle America."[50] President Johnson's concern was based on the fact that he believed Mr. Cronkite expressed the values of the American people, and Cronkite's assessment would be reflected in the people's political judgment at the next election.

Today, the traditional role of democracy's watch dog is challenged by a virtual menagerie of prolific print media, 24-hour TV news programs, and a seemingly limitless Internet capacity that is still struggling to define itself—and perhaps, prefers its role as being undefined. The universality of television, the redefinition of all media as a business enterprise, the liberalization and counter-liberalization of "news people," and the instant legitimization of Internet sources have combined to overwhelm and obscure unbiased information on anything short of the primary source. Pride in objectivity by the "news profession" is sadly lacking in all but a few sources, many of which are not known to or readily available to the general public. As a result, the objectively informed public is dwindling and the misinformed and uninformed publics are growing.

A number of trends contribute to the problem of objectivity and focus in news media. The so-called CNN effect of 24-hour news broadcasting has shorten the time for analysis while the live, persistent coverage has in some regards shaped policy and created news as opposed to reporting it. A highly commercial news media appears to be motivated by the entertainment value or controversy that builds audiences in print or on cable, satellite, and regular television. No clear distinction is made between editorial commentary and objective news reporting. In many cases "facts" are not substantiated and "news stories" are presented without conformation in the rush to be first, entertain, or get airtime. A form of "pack journalism" has emerged where once a story breaks every outlet leaps on the same story, often making the less significant local news, like the O.J. Simpson trial, a major story at the expense of crowding out national or international stories that an uninformed public needs to hear. Even when such news is reported, pundits and sound-bite interviews have replaced serious analysis and discussions, often supplemented with partisan perspectives and half-truths. Many within these media outlets cloak themselves in the virtue of "news and information" to peddle their own agendas. Commercial media is complemented on the Internet by an astounding number of websites catering to every ideological, political, and issue persuasion. The advent of the home computer and the Internet has created a virtual world of formal and informal information and interaction that is undisciplined by any common standard code of conduct. Blogging is a national past time and a primary source for many people's views in regard to national security. As frustrating as this may be, none of this makes the media less essential or less important. Until it has sorted itself out in the marketplace, the national security professional can do little about the actual media, but he can seek every opportunity to promulgate an objective truth.

Getting the truth before the public is further complicated because the sheer capacity and competitive nature of the media environment actively seeks out other views, and preferably conflicting ones. Too often, in the search for audience share, this opportunity is offered without any real understanding of the issues by editors and producers, making anyone's voice appear equally legitimate and representative. At the same time, there is a wide range of individual and collective voices of various persuasions and purposes actively seeking a platform from which to speak. Thus, special interest groups, think tanks, academia, political opponents, and political opportunists stand ready to speak on any aspect of policy and strategy. Both are the people's business and they have a right, and sometimes the obligation, to inform and debate. However, even those who support your policy or strategy can muddy the waters of national consensus. The challenge posed is not to close out the media or shout louder than others, but to formulate and clearly articulate the best policy and strategy so that its merits are obvious to the people. Such a communication environment also suggests that the national security professional must be better informed than others and must seek opportunities to speak out in regard to necessary policy and strategy. Under these circumstances foresight in regard to strategic communications is essential, and policy and strategy should be formulated recognizing the essential role of communication in building consensus at home and acceptance and support abroad.

MULTIPLE-DECISION PROCESSES

As the preceding discussion illustrates VUCA is an inherent part of the domestic environment, and this internal VUCA complicates the decision process in policy and strategy. It is important for the national security professional to understand the nature of this VUCA environment so that he understands the art of the politically possible from a domestic perspective and has an appreciation for what influences decisions and how decisions are actually made. In the book *Essence of Decision* (Revised 1999), authors Graham Allison and Philip Zelikow examined the Cuban missile crisis and looked at how the U.S. and Soviet governments made decisions using three common political science theoretical models to explain what happened: the rational actor, organizational behavior, and governmental politics models. The authors' primary interest is in the different interpretations of the decision process depending on which model is used. The models are promoted by the political analysts because they believe the models represent different ways governments approach decision making. The value of examining and understanding these approaches to the national security professional is in gaining insight into the complexity and realities of strategic decision making so that better policy and strategy can be formulated and better decision making can be facilitated.[51]

Allison and Zelikow's start point was the rational actor model. The rational actor model is essentially a *realpolitik* or realist model. It assumes the state is a unified actor and that the state will act rationally, calculating costs and benefits in responding to threats and opportunities. It is the most common method for explaining state decisions. Since it is rational and unified, the state's decisions will be based on expected value-maximizing—the decision with the highest payoff is always selected. What troubled Allison about this model as a sole explanation of decision making was that an imaginative political scientist could explain any choice as maximizing value, and often ignored a lot of facts to make the analysis fit the rational actor model.[52] In other words, this model does not explain all government decisions or every aspect of any one decision.

As one alternative to the rational actor, the authors used an organizational behavior model to examine the same event. In this model when governments are confronted with a crisis, instead of looking at the whole, the government breaks it down into its component parts and partials it out to different departments and agencies—such as defense and state. The organizations look at it through their organizational lenses—applying different cultures, logic, capacities, and routines—sometimes creating dysfunctional interactive complexity that expends resources without ever conducting a proper strategic appraisal and developing optimal policy or strategy alternatives. Organizations then tend to resort to what they know and adapt existing plans to "fit" the issue. As a consequence decision makers tend to accept the first proposal that adequately addresses the issue instead of examining all the possible alternatives and selecting the best—"satisficing" instead of optimizing.[53]

As a third alternative, the two authors used the governmental politics model. The basic premise of this model is that the leaders who sit atop government's departments and agencies are individual players in a competitive game of politics. The game is about power. Power is influence measured by impact on an issue. Power is associated with charisma, personality, skills of persuasion, and personal ties. The game is played according to politics and established rules, practices, and processes defined in the Constitution, laws, tradition, and executive policy. The power game explains in large part why in the interagency process resolved issues resurface at the principals' level. Players bargain or negotiate along known patterns of rules and behaviors based on their positions and power in the hierarchy of government. Players may share the same goals but their backgrounds and interests lead to different preferred solutions to issues. There are many actors, and they are driven not by a consistent set of strategic objectives or even by the crisis issue, but by a number of different issues and their own conceptions of national, organizational, and personal goals. Their negotiation within the decision group leads to the decision—for better or worst.[54]

In such a decision environment the president needs to build consensus even if he knows what he wants to do. Key leaders and other players form a central circle around the president in a crisis or for a significant decision. Membership in the circle may be by position or the nature of the issue, or individuals may maneuver their way into the circle. Successive, concentric circles surround the inner group consisting of lower officials in the executive branch, the press, NGOs, and the public. Struggles in the outer circles affect decision dynamics in the central circle. To understand decisions you have to understand the interaction in all the circles and the relationship to each other in affecting the inner circle. The inner circle is a distinct decision group. Groups function differently from individuals and while such a group has powerful advantages in bringing diversity and alternatives to decision making, there are known pitfalls such as groupthink, in which harmony in the group is more important than critically examining alternative policy options. Presidents who surround themselves with, and rely on, yes-men or likeminded individuals are naturally exposed to more limited alternatives. Other dynamics are also at work in the inner power circle. People who offend others with widely divergent alternatives risk loss of influence. If the president appears to have already made up his mind, few will offer alternatives and risk their power relationship with him and within the circle. People also play based on a variety of motivations and justifications such as: parochial priorities and perceptions; differences about national goals and interests; organizational stakes and stands; deadlines; interpretations of issues; and perceived individual power. Where an individual is in an organizational hierarchy, how he and his organization are affected by the issue, and how he can influence the decision often determines how he plays.[55]

The domestic environment description preceding the discussion of decision making substantiates to a large degree the validity of these models—what the theorists have described in regard to policy and strategy decision making does correlate to practice. There is no argument here that one model for decision making is better than another. In fact, any model could be dominant in any administration at different times, and most of the time elements of all three are active at the same time, even if one is predominant. Collectively they contribute to the phenomena of internal VUCA. The national security professional that understands this is better prepared to contribute to formulation of proper and practical policy and strategy, and less likely to be disappointed in some of the decision processes in regard to them. If the theory does not account for the practice being observed, then the professional should find or develop a theory that fits, because understanding the functioning decision-making process is critical to success. The best policy or strategy is meaningless to the good of the state if it is not adopted and successfully implemented.

CONCLUSION

The domestic environment is part of the strategic environment and is characterized by its own VUCA. Consequently, the internal–external dialectic described earlier can also be applied to the state's domestic environment and its actors to assess the potential multiordered effects of various policy options and strategic alternatives at home. National security professionals need to understand the domestic environment, how it acts and interacts within itself, and how it will interact with the international environment in order for these professionals to formulate proper policy and strategy and ensure its adoption and successful implementation. Other states may have different internal dynamics but as the duality of the internal–external dialectic suggests, strategy that is not founded solidly in the domestic environment will, in the long run, experience issues of acceptability, feasibility, and public support, even if initially these all appear evident. Therefore, it is essential as part of the strategic appraisal to assess domestic environments in considering other actors, and to understand your own internal environment's dynamics. In democracies both the decision maker and the population must be convinced of the appropriateness of a policy or strategy. National will must be built and sustained by the rational expression of an acceptable logic—ends, ways, and means—and an unambiguous and truthful answer as to why it is necessary. Even then, public support cannot be assumed and a strategic communications concept for sustaining it over time is an inherent consideration for strategy formulation and a key leadership responsibility.

8

The Strategic Appraisal

Nothing is more terrible than activity without insight.

—Thomas Carlyle

Policy and strategy formulation is both an art and a science. As earlier pointed out the latter is important because it suggests that the astute national security professional at any level can apply himself to the study of theory and practice, learn how to think at the strategic level, and participate in the successful formulation and implementation of policy or strategy. Yet, despite the wide availability of theory and historical analysis of policy and strategy both remain problematic in formulation and implementation. With the wisdom of Sun Tzu, Carl von Clausewitz, and others at hand, why do so many policies and strategies fail to meet the test of reality when executed? How can a policy or strategy's fallacies be so obvious in failure, but unrecognized in formulation? The answer is that many are flawed in their formulation because the policymakers and strategists do not see what is important in regard to the interest they are trying to serve. They fail to conduct a proper strategic appraisal and do not determine and make appropriate use of the strategic factors on which the future hinges. Consequently, their policies and strategies are founded on wrong or inappropriate premises. Seeing what is really important is the keystone of a successful policy or strategy. Focusing on irrelevant, false, transient, or easily averted factors, or completely failing to see the real key factors, makes both less adequate, cedes significant advantages to others, requires excessive adaptation and costs, or could lead to catastrophic failure. The purposes of the strategic appraisal are the proper identification of interests and their levels of intensity and the selection of the key strategic factors. This chapter provides a construct and perspectives for getting at these critical elements for strategy formulation. In doing so, it also provides insights for policy formulation.

The ultimate purpose of all strategy is to produce specific effects in the strategic environment that advance or protect the state's interests. National leadership uses strategy to guide interaction with other states or actors—foreign and domestic—and the possibilities of the future to advance the state's well-being. As previously discussed, the strategic environment is inclusive, consisting of the facts, context, conditions, relationships, trends, issues, threats, opportunities, and interactions that influence the success of the state in relation to the physical world, other states and actors, chance, and the possible futures—all of the factors that affect or potentially affect the well-being of the state and the way the state pursues that well-being. The strategic environment acts and reacts in regard to the interplay of continuities and change, seeking to maintain its current equilibrium or to find a new balance. In doing this, it does not necessarily act and react in a direct cause-and-effect manner, but it does behave in a holistic manner. Since in this environment some things are known (predictable), some are probable, some are possible, some are plausible, and some remain simply unknown, what the strategist chooses to act on or in regard to is paramount—everything flows from it. Good strategy formulation is founded in the strategic appraisal process and the proper selection and use of the key strategic factors to determine the right calculation of ends (objectives), ways (concepts), and means (resources) for the strategic situation.[1] The specific purpose of the strategic appraisal is to quantify and qualify what is known, believed to be known, and unknown about the environment and then determine what is important in regard to the state's interests and policy and strategy formulation.

Through constant study, analysis, and evaluation the strategist maintains a holistic world view that gives meaning and context to his understanding of the strategic environment and the forces of continuity and change. Consequently, the policymaker or strategist's *weltanschauung* is both an objective view of the current environment and an anticipatory appreciation of the implications of continuities and change within it for his nation's future well-being. He fully appreciates that the strategic environment possesses the characteristics of a system of systems and exhibits some of the attributes of chaos theory.[2] The strategist accepts that the future is not predictable, but believes it can be influenced and shaped toward more favorable outcomes. His *weltanschauung* makes the strategist sensitive to the balance within the strategic environment as well as what national interests are and the threats, challenges, and opportunities in regard to them. Such a holistic world view is an essential prerequisite for a proper strategic appraisal—the identification

Figure 8.1 Linear View of the Strategic Appraisal Process.

and statement of national interests, the relative importance of various interests, the assessment of available information, the determination of factors that affect the advancement or protection of the interests, and the selection of the key strategic factors leading to the ends, ways, and means of strategy. Examining the discreet steps of the strategic appraisal linearly as portrayed in Figure 8.1 above helps illustrate the various processes, but in practice it, like strategy formulation, is iterative.

The existence of the strategist's *weltanschauung* suggests that the strategist is constantly appraising the strategic environment—and this is an appropriate interpretation of the author's intent—but a new, focused strategic appraisal is conducted when circumstances demand a new strategy or the review of an existing strategy is undertaken. Understanding the stimulus or the requirement for the strategy is the first step in the strategic appraisal. It provides the strategist's motivation, but it will ultimately lend legitimacy, authority, and impetus to the appraisal and strategy formulation processes and the subsequent implementation of the strategy. It answers in part the "why question" in strategy.

The levels and kinds of strategy used within the state fall within different realms. Realms reflect both the hierarchical nature of strategy and its comprehensiveness, thereby allowing the state's leadership to delegate responsibility for strategy at different levels and in different domains while maintaining span of control over a complex process. The strategic appraisal focuses on serving that realm of strategy undertaken—both the kind and level. For example, the term Grand Strategy encompasses both level and

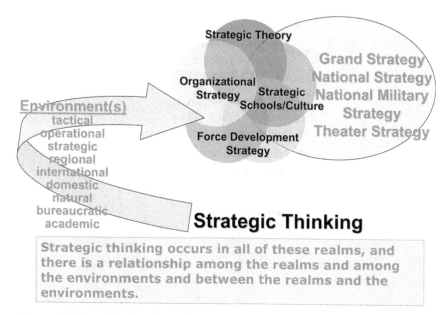

Figure 8.2 The Relationship of Realms of Strategy within the Environment.

kind, implying an overarching strategy that integrates the use of all the state's power in service of all the state's interests. National strategies are at the national level, but they may apply to all elements of power and the associated departments and agencies as the National Security Strategy does or may focus on one element as is the case with the National Military Strategy. Strategies may also have a regional focus, a force developmental focus, an organizational focus, and other foci as illustrated in Figure 8.2.

Thinking about the kind and level of strategy helps develop specificity in the articulation of interests and better focuses the strategy in regard to this desired end-state. It also clarifies and assigns responsibility, authority, and accountability. Nonetheless, the strategist at every level and in every domain must adhere to strategic theory and maintain a holistic perspective.

Donald E. Nuechterlein, in *America Overcommitted: United States National Interests in the 1980's*, describes *national interests* as the perceived needs and desires of a sovereign state in relation to other sovereign states that constitute its external environment.[3] The *DOD Dictionary of Military Terms* defines national security interests as: "The foundation for the development of valid national objectives that define US goals or purposes. National security interests include preserving US political identity, framework and institutions; fostering economic well-being; and bolstering international order supporting the vital interests of the United States and its allies."[4] The nature of the strategic environment, as this book has developed it in regard to the development of policy and strategy, suggests a more generalized definition, such as "the perceived needs and desires of a sovereign state in relation to other sovereign states, non-state actors, and chance and circumstances in an emerging strategic environment expressed as desired end-states." This broader definition encapsulates the dynamism of a strategic environment in which multiple actors, chance, and interaction play, and both external and internal components are recognized. Interests are expressed as general or particular desired end-states or conditions. For example, "U.S. economic well-being" would be a generalized interest, while "international access to Middle Eastern oil" illustrates a more particular economic interest. While some interests may change over time, general interests such as free trade and defense of the homeland are persistent.

Determining and articulating interests is the second step in the strategic appraisal process. Interests are founded in national purpose. National purpose is essentially a summary of our enduring values, beliefs, and ethics as expressed by political leadership in regard to the present and the future they foresee. At the highest-level political leadership uses policy to identify state interests and provide guidance for subordinate policy and strategy. Such policy may appear as general as a vision statement that proclaims a desired future strategic environment or as a more specific statement of guidance with elements of ends, ways, and means. It is found in various documents, speeches, policy statements, and other pronouncements made on behalf of the government by various officials or provided by leadership as direct guidance for the development of strategy. Policy may be inferred as well as stated. It may be the result of a detailed strategic appraisal or arrived at intuitively. Regardless, state policy flows from the formal and informal political processes and the interpretation of the national purpose in the current and desired future strategic environments. Thus, interests are the general or specific statements of the nation's desired end-states within the strategic environment based on the policymakers' understanding of what best serves national well-being.

Interests may be expressed as physical or non-physical conditions. They may represent continuities or changes—things to be protected, things to be promoted, or things to be created. Interests would logically flow from the policy formulation process, but the nature of the political and bureaucratic environments, particularly in a democracy, can make identifying and clearly articulating interests and their relative importance or intensity a difficult task. As stated above, policy in the real-world appears in many formats, often is not clearly stated, and may not be comprehensive in its statement of interests and guidance for serving interests. It may also come from multiple and contradictory sources, such as the executive or legislative branches, and it may be emerging from the interagency process at the time a strategy is demanded. While strategy is subordinate to policy, the strategist must search out and clarify policy intentions and appropriately identify and articulate interests. In cases where policies or interests conflict and clarification is necessary, the strategist provides appropriate recommendations to the approval authority.

Various methodologies for determining interests and levels of intensity have been proposed by theorists over the years. Sometimes, presidential administrations impose their own methodologies to express categories of interests and their associate levels of intensity. In recent years, course materials at the Senior Service Colleges, such as the U.S. Army War College, have focused on three that are termed core U.S. interests: physical security; promotion of values; and economic prosperity. In the Army War College process model these three interests lead directly to three grand strategic objectives: preserve American security; bolster American economic prosperity; and promote American values.[5] In his much earlier argument, Nuechterlein referred to these "core" interests as categories and listed four: Defense of the Homeland, Economic Prosperity, Favorable World Order, and Promotion of Values. Nuechterlein suggested these four end-states were so general in nature that their primary utility lay in considering them as categories to help organize thinking about interests, and that actual interests must be stated with more specificity to be of any use in policy and strategy formulation. He also noted that such categorization is somewhat artificial, and interests tend to bleed over into other categories.[6] The reader would do well to recognize that Nuechterlein is right in both regards. Specificity is critical to good policy and strategy formulation. Specificity lends clarity as to policy's true intent and aids in the identification of the strategic factors important in regard to the interests. In addition, since in the strategic environment everything is interrelated, greater specificity helps define the nature and context of the interest and clarifies the level and kind of strategy appropriate for addressing it. In spite of numerous other constructs, Nuechterlein's categorization remains more useful because of both its clarity and comprehensiveness.

Interests as statements of desired end-states do not imply intended actions or set objectives—policy and strategy does this. Consequently, interests are stated without verbs or other action modifiers. Interests should be expressed with an appropriate degree of specificity. For example, "access to oil" is an expression of a desired end-state, but is very general. It could apply anywhere in the world. "Access to oil in the Middle East" is a regionally specific interest for the state. "Freedom of navigation in the Persian Gulf" might be an expression of a specifically stated interest in the CENTCOM (U.S. Central Command) theater military strategy. Hence, statements of interests in strategies achieve specificity by word choice, fixing the focus, and narrowing the context. Expression of interests, like most things in strategy, remains a matter of choice, but the strategist should be aware of the fact a choice is being made and the potential implications of his word choices—a matter worthy of deliberation and discussion! Therefore, the right degree of specificity is often achieved through an iterative process in which an interest is articulated and then restated as more is learned about the implications of pursuing that interest.

Specificity in interests serves the multiple purposes of clarifying the intent of policy in different realms, focusing attention on the appropriate strategic factors, enabling better strategy formulation, and helping to identify responsibility, authority, and accountability. For example, a military strategy would logically, but not exclusively, focus on end-states that could be accomplished through the application of the military element of power. Not exclusively so, because as Nuechterlein observed interests tend to bleed over into other categories, and the military instrument may also facilitate accomplishment of diplomatic, economic, or informational focused interests. Hence, an interest such as "a democratic Iraq" was an appropriate, if ambitious expression of an interest for a national security strategy or a national regional strategy prior to the second Iraqi War, but a military strategy might have articulated the interest as "a defeated Iraqi military." Military instruments alone could not guarantee a democratic Iraq. Specificity would have clarified strategy because there were major diplomatic, economic, and informational components essential to the end-state of a democratic Iraq that should also have been more appropriately addressed. United States and coalition military forces could and did militarily defeat the Iraqi military, but they were not prepared or well suited for ensuring a democratic Iraq. Such specificity might have made the disconnect between the end-state and the military instrument more obvious. Strategy is hierarchical in nature and a strategy that promises realization of interests beyond its inherent capabilities courts failure and subverts the proper strategy formulation process. Hence, when success in Iraq was defined in terms of a military strategy, as opposed to a national security strategy, the de facto end-state became regime change as opposed to a democratic Iraq, and important factors relative to diplomatic, economic, and informational components were missed or not appropriately addressed in strategy formulation.

Having determined and articulated the interests, the third step in the strategic appraisal is to determine the interests' level of intensity. Different methodologies and models have also guided the determination and expression of levels of intensity. Both Nuechterlein and Army War College methodologies advocate applying levels of intensity to interests to indicate criticality and priority. Levels of intensity at the Army War College include: Vital, Important, and Peripheral.[7] Nuechterlein labeled the important level as "major" and argued for the existence of a fourth intensity—survival—aimed at those threats or changes that challenged the very existence of the nation as we know it.[8] Dropped from most methodologies with the ending of the Cold War, Nuechterlein's survival level deserves reconsideration in light of the increase of weapons of mass destruction (WMD) proliferation

Survival—If unfulfilled, will result in immediate massive destruction of one or more major aspects of the core national interests.

Vital—If unfulfilled, will have immediate consequence for core national interests.

Important—If unfulfilled, will result in damage that will eventually affect core national interests.

Peripheral—If unfulfilled, will result in damage that is unlikely to affect core national interests.

Figure 8.3 Measures of Levels of Intensity.[9]

among nation-states and the potential access and use of WMD by terrorists. Various actors can now potentially pose an imminent, credible threat of massive destruction to the U.S. homeland if their demands are not met. In a period of globalization, such as the world is currently undergoing, an imminent, credible threat of massive disruption to the transportation and informational systems that under gird national existence and a stable world order may also reach survival intensity. In addition, since the U.S. policymaker and strategist is concerned with how others perceive their interests in appraising the environment and evaluating multiordered effects, this level of intensity has utility. For example, surely in the first Gulf War Kuwait perceived national survival as at risk as Saddam crossed the border. Thus, interests must have specificity relative to the realm of the strategy being formulated and a means to identify criticality and priority in order to provide focus in determining strategic factors and formulating strategy.

Levels of intensity indicate criticality and priority of interests in regard to the well-being of the state. They help the strategist understand the relative importance and urgency among interests but do not imply that any should not be considered or addressed in some manner—all interests are worthy of some level of concern. Levels of intensity suggest relative importance and have temporal, resource, and risk acceptance implications, but the decision to act or how to act in regard to them flows from the whole of the strategy formulation process—not the assignment of the intensity. Intensity levels are transitory in that they are subject to change based on the perception of probability, context, consequences, and urgency associated with them at any time. Intensity is dependent on the context of the strategic situation and the policymaker or strategist's interpretation of the context and the importance of the particulars to national well-being. Figure 8.3 provides the definitions of the four intensity levels of survival, vital, important, and peripheral.[10]

Once the strategist has determined interests and identified levels of intensity, the fourth step in the strategic appraisal is to assess the information relative to the interests. In doing this, the strategist casts a wide net. Information includes facts and data relating to any aspect of the strategic environment in regard to the interest(s), including: both tangible and intangible attributes and knowledge; assumptions; relationships; and interaction. He considers all information from friendly, neutral, and adversarial perspectives, and from objective and subjective perspectives in each case. While his emphasis is logically on his realm of strategy, he applies holistic thinking that looks both vertically and horizontally at other realms and across the environment. From this assessment the strategist will identify and evaluate the strategic factors that affect or potentially affect the interests—whether promoting, hindering, protecting, or threatening them. From his evaluation of the factors he will select the key strategic factors—the factors on which his strategy will be based.

The determination of the key strategic factors and the strategist's choices in regard to them is one of the most poorly understood aspects of strategy formulation. It represents a major shortcoming in theoretical consideration of a strategic mindset. Clausewitz devotes a scant two paragraphs to it in his discussion of military genius, using the French term *coup d'oeil* to describe this attribute. He argues the term has a strategic application and that "the concept merely refers to the quick recognition of a truth that the mind would ordinarily miss or would perceive only after long study and reflection." It is the "inward eye" that leads to sound decisions in a timely manner.[11] What Clausewitz refers to is the ability to see what is really important in the strategic situation and being able to devise a way to act in regard to it. In strategy formulation "what is really important" are called strategic factors—the things that determine or influence the realization of the interest. This is step 5 in the strategic appraisal process. Not all information or facts are strategic factors. Strategic factors have meaning relative to the expressed interests. From these the strategist will determine the key strategic factors on which the success of the strategy potentially rises or falls. The distinctions in information, strategic factors, and key strategic factors are outlined in Figure 8.4 below.

Seeing what is really important flows from a thorough assessment of the realities and possibilities of the strategic environment, tempered with an understanding of its nature and strategic theory. Again, strategy in its essence is about creating a more "favorable future" for the state than might exist if left to chance or the actions of adversaries and others. It is proactive, but not predictive. Thus, in dealing with unknowns and uncertainties of the future, the strategist forecasts from a knowledge and understanding of the systems of the strategic environment—what they are (facts and assumptions) and how they interact (observation, reason, and assumptions) within the various dimensions of interaction. He considers these in terms of continuities and change—thinking in time streams to see how the present

Information	Facts and data relating to any aspect of the strategic environment in regard to the interest(s), including both tangible and intangible attributes and knowledge, assumptions, relationships, and interaction.
Strategic Factors	The things that can potentially contribute or detract causally to the realization of the specified interests or other interests.
Key Strategic Factors	Factors the strategist determines are at the crux of interaction within the environment that can or must be used, influenced, or countered to advance or protect the specified interests.

Figure 8.4 Information and Factors.

can be affected by change and how continuities of the past and changes today may play out in the future. From this assessment the strategist derives the strategic factors—the things that can potentially contribute or detract causally to the realization of the interest. As previously stated, factors may be tangible or intangible, representing any aspect of the environment. The existence of other states and actors, geography, culture, history, relationships, perspectives and perceptions, and facts and assumptions all represent potential factors that must be considered in the strategic appraisal. What the strategist understands they are and what others believe them to be are both important.

Having identified strategic factors, the strategist continues his assessment to determine which are the key strategic factors—step 6 in the strategic appraisal process. Key strategic factors are those critical factors at the crux of interaction within the strategic environment, representing the potential critical points of tension between continuities and change within the system of systems where the strategist may choose to act or must act to realize the interest. In strategy formulation these critical strategic factors are the "keys" to developing an effective strategy, because using, influencing, and countering them is how the strategist creates strategic effects and advances or protects interests. The strategist seeks to change, leverage, or overcome these, in effect modifying or retaining the equilibrium within the strategic environment by setting objectives and developing concepts and marshaling resources to achieve the objectives. When successfully selected and achieved, the objectives create strategic effects that tip the balance in favor of the stated interests. The strategist's assessment of how to best do this is reflected in his calculation of the relationship of ends, ways, and means—the rationally stated output of strategic thought. The calculation and each of its components are based on the strategist's assessment of the relationship among the desired end-state and various key factors. It is his appraisal of the strategic environment and selection of the key strategic factors that sets up the calculation. Too often in strategy development practitioners apply insufficient effort to the identification and use of these key strategic factors and as a consequence what is really important is often overlooked, misidentified, or ill addressed—leading to a less effective or failed strategy.

Hence, the biggest conundrum confronting the strategist in strategy formulation is identifying the key strategic factors. By definition, the strategic environment is big and there is a lot of information and VUCA (volatility, uncertainty, complexity, and ambiguity) in it—the conundrum is to determine what is really important in an overwhelming amount of information and possibilities. How are strategic factors determined? How does the strategist achieve the focus that enables him to disregard the unimportant and not overlook something critical? Of the things deemed strategic factors, how does the strategist choose those that are keys and should be addressed by strategy? How do key strategic factors lead to the rational expression of strategic thinking as ends, ways, and means? The thought processes to answer these questions are the heart of the strategic appraisal. Models and insights offered by theorists and practitioners provide guides to assist and discipline the appraisal process, but it starts with an open mind that seeks inclusive answers to broad questions. From there the strategist applies his strategic thinking competencies to narrow the focus through a successive series of questions and answers that lead to the distillation of the key factors.

Postulating broad questions creates the mindset necessary to see what is important. What are the U.S. interests and levels of intensity are the first questions and are steps 2 and 3 in the process. Factors flow from analysis and synthesis of information relevant to the interests and their intensities. What do I know in regard to facts—actors, geography, culture, history, economics, relationships, perspectives and perceptions, etc.? For example, who else has relevant interests, what are they, and what is the level of intensity? What do I not know, what can I find out, and what must I assume? What presumptions are at work in my thinking or that of others? Where can change be introduced to favorable effect? What or what changes create unfavorable effect? These are big questions and to answer them the strategist draws on his *weltanschauung*, focused individual research and study, and the expertise and counsel of others.

Factors are defined as pertinent facts, trends, threats, conditions, or inferences that imply an affect on the realization of the interest. Thus, factors are not accumulations of information or statements of simple facts. And their scope exceeds that of "facts bearing on the problem" in the problem-solving staff study because they are concerned with what has occurred in the past, what might occur in the future, and multiordered effects of any changes. Factors are distinguished from information by the strategist's assessment of their potential multicausal interdependence with the interest. While some may have a visible direct cause-and-effect relationship, many will be less obvious and their importance lies in their second, third, or further multiordered implications in regard to the interest.

Consequently, factors are stated in such a manner that they show their bearing on the interest. For example, if the stated national interest is "a stable, peaceful China," the fact the Great Wall is 4,000 miles long is interesting, but it is only information and not a factor in regard to the interest, because the wall no longer plays a part in China's internal stability or defense. It is also a fact that the population of China is in excess of 1.3 billion. One could argue that it is a strategic factor because the sheer magnitude of the numbers involved has implications for the stated interest. However, in and of itself, the fact is of little help to the strategist other than no strategy in regard to China could ignore the inferences of such a large population. As stated, it has no real context in regard to the interest. A population-related fact better expressed as a factor potentially affecting the stability interest is: "The Chinese government is struggling to sustain adequate job growth for tens of millions of workers laid off from state-owned enterprises, migrants and new entrants to the work force."[12] This trend could potentially threaten domestic stability in China and has a causal relationship with the interest. If the strategist considered this a key strategic factor, his strategy in regard to China would establish objectives or pursue strategic concepts that mitigated this trend. *The National Security Strategy of the United States of America* (September 2002) sought to influence global peace and domestic stability in China and elsewhere by promoting prosperity and reducing poverty around the world with an objective to "Ignite a New Era of Global Economic Growth Through Free Markets and Free Trade." It argued market economies were better than "command-and-control" economies.[13] The strategy helped encourage China toward a more viable economy and subsequent job creation.[14] Numerous other strategic factors influenced this national strategy, but the growth of the Chinese economy and its successful integration into the American-led global economy did promote a more "stable, peaceful China."

Getting at strategic factors is difficult and ultimately, like most aspects of strategy, the selection of key strategic factors is a matter of choice by the strategist. Sorting through the VUCA of the strategic environment in search of what is really important has intrigued theorists and practitioners throughout history. Clausewitz' reference to *coup d'oeil* acknowledges the difficulty and the rarity of the mindset that can see it.[15] Sun-tzu in the *The Art of War* devotes a chapter, "Initial Estimates," to dealing with VUCA, suggesting a consideration of five factors in order to " . . . evaluate it comparatively through estimations, and seek out its true nature."[16] While these two theorists are focused on war, the need for an appraisal and the difficulty of getting at what is important is equally true of all strategies. In today's strategic environment, the strategist should approach the appraisal from multiple perspectives using his understanding of strategic theory and applying all the strategic-thinking competencies in his collection, analysis, synthesis, and evaluation of the information to determine the strategic factors, and subsequently the key strategic factors. As stated previously, the strategic thinking competencies act as lenses to assist the national security professional in his evaluation of VUCA of the strategic environment, reminding the strategist and others of the dimensions of the intellect that should be applied to seek and sort information and to recognize which factors are key.[17]

Critical thinking processes are applicable to both problem solving and strategic thinking, suggesting a rational way to determine the interest and the related strategic factors. The major components of the process—clarify the concern, evaluate information, evaluate implications, and make decisions/use judgment—lead to an understanding of the facts and considerations relative to the interest and their implications. The assessment of points of view and the clarification of assumptions and inferences, as well as argument analysis and consideration of the impact of biases and traps, when applied to other actors and one's self clarifies what are important in the strategic context internally and externally. By its design, the critical thinking process seeks hard facts, forces consideration of the unknowns and the role of chance, and recognizes that the strategic environment consists of both physical and humanistic systems.[18] It is one thinking lens that has great application in the strategic appraisal process.

Richard E. Neustadt and Ernest R. May in *Thinking in Time: The Uses of History for Decision Makers* also place emphasis on determining all the factors and selecting the key factors as a basis for decision making. While their focus is on issue policy and the terminology does not use the word "factor," their first step in asking for the identification of key elements that are known, unclear, and presumed is obviously focused on determining factors. One insightful approach to this they use is to identify multiple past situations that appear analogous and list similarities and differences. Again, this process logically leads to identifying not only what is known and important in the current situation, but leverages history to get insights into potentially unrecognized factors and relationships among factors. Other steps they recommend help collect information and support the determination of factors and the selection of key strategic factors. Their "Goldberg Rule" asks for the full story of an issue over time. "Time-lines" explores the issue's history for key trend lines, events, and changes getting at what and when. Their "Journalist's Questions" seek answers to the classic questions of where, who, how, and why? In their process for identifying and selecting options, the focus on "what can we do now" leads back to key strategic factors and potential objectives and concepts. "Feasibility," "presumptions," and "patterns and inferences" all suggest ways of sorting information in a manner that identifies what is important. Neustadt and May's concept of "thinking in time" also sheds light on what is important. It connects discrete phenomena over time and is able to relate the connections to potential futures and choices for a desired future—hence this thinking process identifies factors that matter in a strategy seeking a more favorable future.[19] Thinking in time is a disciplined process that helps mitigate uncertainty, complexity, and ambiguity.

The other strategic thinking competencies also offer insights into how to think of and identify strategic factors. Systems thinking focuses on comprehending the whole, but the process identifies systems, interdependence among systems, individual aspects of particular systems in regard to their roles or functions within the whole, and the effects of any changes induced on the whole.[20] It is synthesis centric, rather than analysis focused, asking how things come together as opposed to breaking them apart and addressing them individually as a planner might. Creative thinking processes offer new and different ways of looking at information and considering relationships among data, actors, and events. They identify, explain, and help see the importance of factors in innovative and holistic ways.[21] Ethical thinking processes force the examination of moral factors.[22] From each perspective and process, information and insights are acquired and what is important in regard to interests is revealed. The strategist seeks factors relative to his own state's interests, factors relative to his adversaries' interests, factors relative to others' interests, and factors relative to the physical world and chance—looking for what is important that must be addressed or affords an opportunity to serve the state's interests. By disciplining one's thinking to consider the five different lenses the strategist precludes blindspots and creates opportunities for looking at things differently; thereby increasing the probability of seeing what is important.

Structural analysis models can also assist in sorting what is important within the vast information available and lead to the identification of the key strategic factors. One structure to use in information's analysis is to look at the information from the perspective of the elements of power. Facts or trends that indicate or affect balance and relationships in power are potential strategic factors. Hence, focusing on the natural and social determinants of power of the various actors serves as a filter for sorting through the overwhelming volume of information to see what is important. The elements of power are listed in Figure 8.5. Such a filter works because there are casual and interdependence relationships among interests, power, and strategy that become apparent under disciplined consideration.

Natural Determinants	Social Determinants
• Geography	• Economic
• Population	• Military
• Natural Resources	• Political
	• Socio-Psychological

Figure 8.5 Elements of Power Structural Lens.

Power is relative, dynamic, and contextual and the examination and weighing of information in regard to power reveal relevant factors and suggest which are key.[23] Again, the strategist considers it from the multiple perspectives of self, adversaries, others, the physical world, and chance.

Since the strategic environment is a system of systems, and people and other human entities depicted in Figure 8.6 are part of the interaction, an actor structural analysis is another way to filter information to see what is really important in regard to specific interests. Individual personalities and collective mentalities matter in the pursuit of interests. Here the strategist poses broad questions such as: who is affected by this interest and how; who else shares or opposes this interest and why; how will others act or react in regard to this interest and how and why; and what influences others' actions in regard to this interest and why? Answers to these questions reveal factors that must be considered. As discussed earlier, Spanier and Wendzel, in the classic textbook *Games Nations Play*, offer a variation of this structural approach with their three levels of analysis: international system level, actor level, and decision-maker level.[24] Examining the interdependence of these three levels from the various actors' perspectives in a structural-analysis approach provides further insights into the important factors.

Since factors relate strategy to the interests and a proper focus of strategy is interaction, the dimensions of interaction in the strategic environment are another important information filter. In this construct, the strategist uses

• Individual	• Movements
• Leadership	• States
• Groups	• International Business Organizations
• Organizations	• Private Organizations
• Institutions	• International Governmental Organizations
• Interagency/ Bureaucracy	
• Society/Culture	

Figure 8.6 An Actor Structural Analysis Approach.

- **People**
- **Society**
- **Culture**
- **Politics**
- **Ethics**
- **Economics and logistics**
- **Organization**
- **Administration**
- **Information and intelligence**

- **Strategic theory and doctrine**
- **Technology**
- **Operations**
- **Command**
- **Geography**
- **Friction/chance/uncertainty**
- **Adversary**
- **Time**

Figure 8.7 Gray's Dimensions of Strategy.[25]

the dimensions as lenses to focus attention on what is important amongst the prolificacy of information. These dimensions are in play to a greater or lesser extent at all times. As discussed earlier, Colin S. Gray identifies some seventeen of these dimensions as depicted in Figure 8.7, but acknowledges there may be many more. Factors derived from analysis using these dimensions must be considered individually and holistically—that is each distinctly but at the same time in context with each other. Since particular dimensions play a greater role or are more critical at particular times in history, the strategist must be attuned to this potential and the fact none of the dimensions can be ignored over time. A dimension of strategy approach is a valid methodology for identifying what is important in regard to an interest because it allows the question: "what is important relative to this interest in this dimension and how does it interact with the whole of the environment?"

The internal–external duality construct developed in the international environment chapter to consider multiordered effects is another valuable method for filtering information. Ultimately the strategist is seeking to synthesize the duality down to the international–domestic interaction and assess the implications for strategy. When properly applied, the internal–external duality assists the strategist to conduct a thorough appraisal and maintain a holistic view. In the international environment the internal perspective focuses on identifying and evaluating localized factors' potential for affecting the specific interest—information that is clearly within the scope of the strategy being formulated. It asks the strategist to consider those factors that have a direct bearing or relationship. For example, in a regional strategy all the internal regional factors, such as actors, facts, issues, trends, and assumptions that have a potential bearing on the interest, are evaluated. For a specific-issue strategy all the factors that directly affect the interest are considered, such as other actors who have a direct interest or trends that obviously have direct bearing. For a global strategy, the focus is on the major factors that directly affect the realization of the stated interests and the balance of power.

The external factor perspective in the international environment reminds the strategist to broaden his scope and consider other information in the strategic environment for factors that might act indirectly to influence the realization of the specified interest or interests. For a regional strategy it begs the question of what actors outside the region may have an interest in the region or an external interest that relates to your success in the region. It also asks what challenges, threats, trends, and opportunities in the rest of the world may affect the realization of your regional interest? For an issue-oriented strategy, it might ask what other not issue-specific trends or actors may affect realization of the specified U.S. interests and under what conditions? For a global strategy the external factors sought are the indirect influences and wild cards that may affect realization of the interests. Examples are: what is the role of international public opinion; how will our allies' domestic public opinion influence their support; how will actors not directly affected react to our use of different types of power and why? This construct encourages the strategist to consider multiordered effects in the international environment.

Domestic factors remind the strategist to consider what domestic issues, political and organizational agendas, public opinion, and events may help, hinder, or preclude the realization of an interest. Following the construct, internal factors are those things in the domestic environment that directly affect the realization of an interest. The types of broad questions might include: what values are affected and how do they impact; are there existing policies and strategies in regard to this interest; what special interest groups might become involved; how does the press and the public relate to this interest; what outcomes are acceptable or unacceptable to the American people; and what resources are available? In the domestic environment external factors are those things that might indirectly influence the realization of the interest and beg questions like: what other domestic situations or priorities may affect this interest; are there partisan political concerns; is it an election year; what is the state of the economy; and how much credibility or political capital does the president possess? Again, the purpose of the construct is to evaluate for multiordered effects, and it is an iterative process. Each new factor begs the question of how it interacts with other domestic and international factors.

From his assessment and synthesis of the information, the strategist determines the relevant factors—facts, issues, assumptions, presumptions, threats, and opportunities—that *act or interact to affect the interest*. These factors are written as simple factual statements in a manner that makes clear how they affect and if they assist or hinder U.S. interests. From this broad understanding and list of factors, the strategist develops a refined list of key strategic factors by asking a new series of questions. What can most likely detract from or preclude the realization of the interest? What best supports or can be leveraged to realize the interest? What does policy guidance allow or preclude? What assumptions are inherent to my understanding of the situation and realization of the interests? Can these assumptions be made factual? What changes in facts or assumptions would affect the realization of interests and how? What role does chance play—are there wild cards? These questions lead to the key strategic factors—the factors the strategy must account for or that the strategist thinks provides the key to successful pursuit of the interest.

The strategist is now poised to formulate a specific strategy. Using the strategic appraisal framework he applied strategic thinking competencies and various models to clarify interests and levels of intensity, culled out strategic factors relevant to the realization of the interests from an over-abundance of information, and further refined this broad list of factors into a list of key strategic factors on which to base a strategy. However, the strategic appraisal framework has done much more than this. It has immersed the strategist in the strategic environment from the perspective of specific national interests. It has identified what is important relative to those interests, forced the strategist to distinguish between fact and assumption, and alerted him to the consequences of change. Thus, the framework focuses the strategy formulation process on the key strategic factors, suggests where flexibility is needed, and how strategy might be made adaptive. Further, it provides indicators for potential future issues and prepares the strategist for considering changes in strategy.

Once the first six steps of the strategic appraisal are complete, the strategist seeks to act on or use the key strategic factors to influence the strategic environment favorably without inadvertently creating other un-favorable effects in the strategic environment—reflected as step 7 in the linear depiction of the process. This is the transition to strategy formu-lation proper—the articulation of ends, ways, and means. These factors suggest suitable objectives, suggest or limit concepts, and identify resource requirements and availability. It is the key strategic factors that both sug-gest and bound the feasibility, acceptability, and suitability (FAS) in strategy formulation. The assessment of the factors also provides the basis for the consideration of risk in a strategy. Through his formulation of appropri-ate ends, ways, and means to manipulate the factors and take advantage of the opportunities or avoid the negative possibilities, the strategist cre-ates the favorable strategic effects leading to the realization of the interest. Which factors to act upon, what objectives to set to create favorable strate-gic effects, what concepts to use to achieve those objectives without adverse effects, and what resources to provide to implement the concepts are all choices made in strategy formulation from the knowledge gained in the strategic appraisal. As depicted in Figure 8.8, to the extent this is done well, more favorable effects are created leading to the closer realization of the interest.

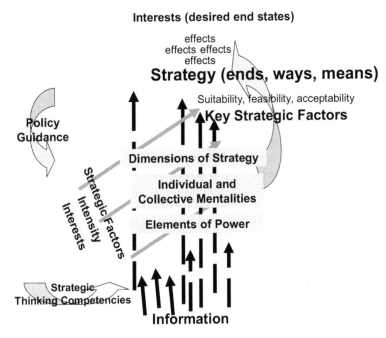

Figure 8.8 The Strategic Appraisal and the Formulation of Strategy.

CONCLUSION

The strategic appraisal framework as described herein is a linear and "scientific" portrayal of the importance and determination of key strategic factors in strategy formulation. In practice the strategic environment's VUCA nature requires non-linear and iterative thinking and the application of all the strategic thinking competencies—as well as a constantly evolving *weltanschauung* that melds art and science. A strategist or national security professional might find the policymaker asking for a strategic appraisal before providing policy guidance, and, of course, must always be prepared to reexamine interests and earlier conclusions in light of new information. Theorists acknowledge that chance or superior thinking by adversaries can thwart the best strategy—others always have the choice to act. However, the study of practice suggests that too often policies and strategies fail to measure up to the realities they encounter because the national security professional did not do the hard and comprehensive research and thinking required of a proper strategic appraisal. In essence, the policymaker or strategist lacked the eye for what was really important and failed to base his strategy on the key strategic factors in the strategic environment with which he was confronted.

The strategic appraisal framework serves to discipline the national security professional's thought process and codify its output. Like all theory, it educates, but does not dictate—the human mind must make the choices. Yet, through education, it leads to potentially better appraisals and a more careful consideration of what the interests are and the factors to be considered in regard to them. Through codification, it allows for critical review and a shared understanding of how a strategy is expected to work. As such, the framework is a useful tool, but a healthy weltanschauung is essential to retain the proper perspective on the validity of a strategy and to recognize whether and when modification or a new strategy is necessary. Theory can aid the practice of strategic *coup d'oeil* and strategy formulation by offering a framework for identifying and considering the relevant factors, but the policymaker or strategist's choice of what to do, how to do it, and the resources to be made available remains a creation of the active intellect.

9

Strategy Formulation

Power is a means, not an end.[1]
—Williamson Murray and Mark Grimsley

Strategy, as has often been stated herein, is both an art and a science. Again, strategic theory and all the strategic thinking competencies are called into play in the development and rational expression of the strategic trinity of objectives, concepts, and resources. No matter how easily it lends itself to clever labeling and packaging, strategy must always be the product of deep and iterative thinking. It is never a power point slide project or product. Strategy must be communicated carefully in specific words—words have meaning and meaning matters in strategy! In addition, while the trinity is at the heart of effective strategy, ends, ways, and means convey much less if the strategy document does not clearly articulate *why* they are important in regard to the specific national interests and the greater national purpose. It is these connections that help others understand what the strategy is really seeking to do and alerts the system when strategy may need to be modified or replaced. And while policy and strategy have valid hierarchical positions and purposes in the affairs of the state, strategic thinking applies to both policy and strategy and, hence, to strategists, policymakers, and other national security professionals who can all apply the thought processes offered here.

In its holistic synthesis and evaluation of the strategic environment the strategic appraisal identifies what is important in regard to the national purpose, both internally and externally. It yields an understanding of what the national interest is for the realm of strategy being addressed, expresses the national interest in terms of specific interests and levels of intensity and the logic of "why," and determines the key strategic factors relevant to the interests. Formulating a strategy as a rational statement of ends, ways, and means is the next step. Theory and practice provide insights into how to develop and articulate the ends, ways, and means of strategy, and the relationships among them. Any strategy's internal logic must be tested in terms of feasibility, acceptability, and suitability criteria. In addition, all strategy has risk inherent to it, and the decision maker should be apprised of the risk: theory and practice provides criteria for risk assessment. This chapter examines the development of ends, ways, and means, and how to test the logic and risk of strategy.

DEVELOPMENT OF STRATEGIC OBJECTIVES

In strategy formulation, getting the objectives (ends) right matters most! Too often in strategy development, too little time is spent on consideration of the appropriate objectives in the context of the desired policy, national interests, and the environment. Yet, it is the identification and achievement of the right objectives that creates the desired strategic effect. Objectives are the true focus of strategy formulation and, if not properly selected and articulated, a proposed strategy is fundamentally flawed and cannot be effective. If the wrong objectives are identified, the concepts and resources serve no strategic purpose. Thus, the logic of strategy argues objectives are primary even though concepts and resources are also crucial to success—action and costs are subordinate to purpose in strategy. Yet, in strategy formulation efficiency is often confused with effectiveness by both strategists and leadership. Strategy must reflect a preference for effectiveness. In this regard, objectives are concerned with doing the right things. Concepts are concerned with doing things right. Resources are concerned with costs. Objectives determine effectiveness; concepts and resources are measures of efficiency. A lack of efficiency increases the cost of success, but a lack of effectiveness precludes success. Ultimately strategy's success can be measured only in terms of the degree to which its objectives are accomplished. Thus, again, efficiency is subordinate to effectiveness.[2] At the point where constraints on concepts or resources risk achievement of the objectives, the strategy is in question.

For the nation–state, strategy and strategic objectives are derived from policy consideration of protecting or advancing national interests within the context of the strategic environment as it is, and as it may become. In the past, security policy has largely focused on the international strategic environment in regard to national security needs. The domestic strategic environment was less identified with national security concerns. "Globalization" and its derivatives, such as an integrated world economy and the global war on terrorism, have forced a general acceptance that the concept of internal and external strategic security environments is less distinct than in the past.

Within the United States, such realization has subordinated national security strategy to a larger grand strategy concerned with both domestic and international issues in many current theorists' thinking. In either case, strategy is driven by national interests at the state level, and the strategist must be considerate of both the external and internal components of the strategic environment in the development of strategy.

The strategist must understand national interests and policy in order to formulate appropriate strategy. Given the complexity of the strategic environment, the strategist must be holistic in his consideration, and understand and apprise the policymaker of the interaction and conflict between a particular policy and larger interests or other policy. Lower-level leaders may state more definitive guidance as policy but such policy is subordinate to higher-level policy and strategy. Strategists at lower organizational levels must understand comprehensively interests, higher policy and strategy, and their own guidance to formulate subordinate strategies. In all cases, strategy is subordinate to policy and hierarchical in application. Nonetheless, the strategy development process by its nature evaluates the appropriateness, practicality, and consequences of policy, and, thus informs policy of the art of the possible and the costs and benefits of achievement or failure.

For example, military subordination to civilian policymakers is a recurring and sensitive issue in civil–military relations within the United States. The political leadership and the American people expect their military to execute the guidance provided by elected officials faithfully. Yet, the American people also demand that their military perform professionally and win the nation's wars. Civil–military relations are not an exclusively American issue. Clausewitz provided a proper perspective on the relationship of the military and policy in *On War*: "The assertion that a major military development or the plan for one, should be a matter of *purely military* opinion is unacceptable and can be damaging. Nor indeed is it sensible to summon soldiers, as many governments do when they are planning for a war, and ask them for *purely military* advice."[3] Policy provides guidance for objectives and use of the instruments of power, but the strategy formulation process logically informs policy. In a democratic society, the military professional must build a relationship with civilian leadership that facilitates the essential two-way communication between policy and strategy. Clausewitz's logic also applies to any relationship between strategy and policy or superior to subordinate policy and strategy. If superior policy fails to guide, asks the improbable, or unnecessarily confines strategy, and it is not resolved, the level of risk associated with the strategy goes up.

In the world of the strategist, strategy can be demanded when inadequate or no-policy guidance has been provided. In such a case, the strategist's responsibility is to seek policy clarification from leadership. Often this is best done by recommending alternative policy choices based on an assessment of interests in relation to strategic circumstances—a necessary assessment for strategy formulation also. The distinction is that the policy alternatives are derived directly from the interests. Both policy and strategy should be consistent with the protection or advancement of overall state interests in the strategic environment. It is the responsibility of the strategist and other national security professionals to identify all the viable alternatives.

Strategy seeks to protect or advance a particular interest, or the general interest, of the state within the strategic environment relative to other actors, circumstances, and chance in accordance with guidance provided by policy. In doing this, strategy uses the strategic appraisal to determine the relevant factors—facts, issues, threats, and opportunities—that act or interact to affect the interest. Strategy seeks to act on or use these factors to influence the strategic environment favorably without inadvertently creating other unfavorable circumstances within the environment. These factors are the primary focus of strategy; their relationship to the interest and policy guidance leads to appropriate objectives and concepts—what is to be accomplished and how to use the state's instruments of power to accomplish the objectives. Instruments of power may be used singularly or in combination; and directly or indirectly. Given the complex and chaotic nature of the environment, defining the right objectives for desired strategic effect, developing a proper concept, and providing resources are all formidable tasks.

Since strategy is hierarchical, the strategist must understand the level of strategy at which he is working, the nature of the strategic environment at his level in regard to internal and external factors, and the comprehensiveness of strategy—the consequences of his choices in regard to other levels of strategy. With this in mind, the strategist can develop objectives. Strategic objectives may be derived from policy, higher levels of strategy, or the independent analysis of the strategic environment. The primary question in determining objectives is this: What end(s), if accomplished, will create the desired strategic effect in support of policy or interests without detrimental collateral effects?

Objectives (ends) explain "what" is to be accomplished. They flow from a consideration of the interest, which is expressed as a desired end-state, and the key strategic factors in the environment affecting the realization of this desired end-state. Objectives are bounded by policy guidance, higher strategy, the nature of the strategic environment, and the capabilities and limitations of the instruments of powers available. Objectives are selected to create strategic effect. Strategic objectives, if accomplished, create or contribute to creation of strategic effects that lead to the achievement of the desired end-state at the corresponding level of strategy, ultimately serving national interests. In strategy, objectives are expressed with explicit verbs (e.g., deter war, promote regional stability, destroy Iraqi armed forces). Explicit verbs force the strategist to consider and qualify what is to be accomplished and help establish the parameters for the use of power.

A number of problems plague the strategic community in regard to the development of objectives. Objectives too seldom receive the depth of thought and reflection they merit. The objectives establish the parameters of all that follows. Objectives must reflect a thorough understanding of the end-state desired, the nature of the environment, policy guidance, and the multiordered effects required to create the conditions for the end-state. The diversity of outcomes possible in the environment means that the totality of specific results can rarely be predicted at the outset.[4] Strategy, as a matter of principle, must be flexible and adaptable. Thus, strategy cannot be made static by objectives that are too confining. In its formulation, it must focus on "comprehensive" objectives that reflect an understanding of the dynamic nature of the strategic environment and are sufficiently encompassing to allow for change in execution without losing focus on policy or interests. On the other hand, objectives so broad or vague that they can be misinterpreted or fail to provide appropriate direction risk the success of policy. Strategic objectives logically bound, but do not unnecessarily confine subordinate levels.

Strategic objectives maintain their validity, while providing for adaptability and flexibility, by focusing on root purposes and causes. If objectives are set at the strategic level with a focus on root purposes and causes and an appreciation of the nature of the strategic environment (chaos, complexity, human nature, chance, friction, etc.), they are logically of sufficient breadth to provide the necessary adaptability and flexibility to confront the unforeseen. In turn, they also logically broaden the scope of consideration for ways and means—further enhancing the preconsideration of adaptability. Most strategists make the objectives too narrow and precise, pushing their thinking down to the planning level. At the planning level, exactness of detail is more valued because it can be quantified and made actionable. Such detail works in the planning realm because of the reduced scope and greater certainty. Planning-level objectives elevated to the strategic level are more susceptible to failure as a result of the scope and chaotic nature of the strategic environment, which exponentially multiplies possibilities for friction and asymmetric reactions by others. In strategy, the focus is on clarity of objectives appropriate for the level, not prescribing detailed instructions for lower levels. Strategic objectives directly serve the strategic purpose—the desired end-state.

Simply put, if the strategic objective is to win the war, then losing a battle is regrettable but does not necessarily preclude achievement of the strategic objective. The state can seek additional battles or apply other instruments of power. On the other hand, if the objective is to not lose a battle, then the state has been denied its strategic objective as soon as a single battle is lost. The strategy has failed, producing different repercussions in the internal and external components of the strategic environment, even if the war is ultimately won. The "win-every-battle" strategy has also confined its use of power to the military instrument. In modern war, winning battles is a planning objective; winning wars is a strategic objective. Strategy focuses on root purposes and causes. To do otherwise is to divert focus and power, lessening probabilities for success, and increasing the probability of unintended second- and third-order effects. This eventuality appears evident in the U.S. national-level strategic approach in the second Iraq war.

While the Bush administration has been somewhat ambiguous on root purposes in the second Iraq war, one expressed root purpose in going to war with Iraq was to effect a regime change in Baghdad so that international terrorists would be denied state sponsorship and potential weapons of mass destruction. A number of "strategic" objectives emerged from this purpose: (1) defeat Iraqi military forces in war, (2) remove Saddam Hussein from power, and (3) establish a new democratic Iraqi regime. One could postulate that the first objective, defeat Iraqi military forces, was inappropriate as a national security-level objective and should have been subordinated by locating it at the theater military level. In practice, these objectives were sought sequentially. Through its elevation and sequential expression, the defeat of Iraq military forces became the focal point of the strategy when, in fact, the key objective and point of focus should have been the establishment of a new democratic regime, with the military defeat of Iraqi forces and the removal of Saddam Hussein expressed as acceptable strategic outcomes in guiding subordinate levels.

As a consequence of this misdirected focus, the military objective occupied the time and talent of the policymakers and national-level military leadership with consequent neglect of the third objective. While this proposition is debatable, it is clear that the presumption of the strategy was that the defeat of the Iraq military would lead directly to the accomplishment of the other objectives. In actual fact, more thought and a more intense focus and effort on how to achieve the democratic regime objective was needed. The inappropriate elevation of the objective and the sequencing also illustrate the mind-set that inflicting military defeat is essential to the achievement of the other two objectives. Again, this may or may not have been true, but the point is that defeat of the Iraq military forces was an appropriate focus for a lower level of strategy or planning. The closer you approach planning, the easier the conceptualization becomes—it quantifies and can be made more precise. People prefer certainty and migrate toward it—it is more comfortable. Strategy deals with ambiguity and uncertainty. Most people are uncomfortable with these and seek to move toward the known at the expense of improperly assessing and thus jeopardizing the recognition and achievement of the proper objectives.

DEVELOPING STRATEGIC CONCEPTS

Strategic concepts (ways) explain "how" the objectives are to be accomplished by the employment of the instruments of power. Instruments of power are the manifestation of the elements of power (the state's resources) in action. Thus a naval blockade might be the instrument to apply the economic and military elements of power. Strategic concepts link resources to the objectives by addressing *who does what, where, when, and why to explain how an objective will be achieved.* Here, think of the "what" as the "little what," describing what you want the subordinate levels to do as part of the strategic concept. The strategic objective is the "big what" that must be accomplished to create the specific effects in the environment. The consideration of concepts reveals if in fact the objective can be accomplished with the resources available, or if more resources must be sought. It also provides the opportunity for creative strategic thinking to bridge supposed disconnects in objectives and resources, perhaps, the highest form of strategic art. Since concepts convey action, they often employ verbs in their construction, but are descriptions of "how" the objective of a strategy is to be accomplished. However, the verb choice is important, as is word choice throughout the articulation of strategy. Word choices imply levels of effort and degrees of acceptability. Strategic concepts provide direction and boundaries for subordinate strategies and planning—words matter! A strategic concept must be explicit enough to provide planning guidance to those selected to implement and resource it, but not so detailed as to eliminate creativity and initiative at subordinate strategy and planning levels. Logically, concepts become more specific at lower levels as details are pushed down to the subordinate strategy and planning levels, but the complexity of the strategic environment is resolved at the responsible strategic level.

Strategic concepts are often the central focus of a strategy. Some would label the concept as the strategy, but strategy always consists of ends, ways, and means—and the focus is on how they interact synergistically within the strategic environment to produce the desired effects. Some concepts are so accepted that their names have been given to specific strategies. Containment, forward defense, assured destruction, and forward presence are illustrative. In actual practice, these strategies had specific objectives and resources associated with them, and the concept was better developed than the short title might infer. Good strategy is an integral whole of the right objectives pursued through appropriate concepts and supported with the necessary resources. Wrong objectives supported by brilliant concepts will not protect or advance national interests.

Concept development can be understood best as a competitive enterprise. Good ideas and capabilities compete for consideration and adoption and/or adaptation and inclusion. More than at the tactical, or even the operational level, strategic success comes from diversity of thought and approaches that leads to a full consideration of the complexity involved and development of simple but comprehensive concepts that ensure accomplishment of the objectives. Few strategic objectives are accomplished with only one element or instrument of power, and strategy must consider, prioritize, and assign dominate and subordinate roles to the elements and instruments of power in the concepts and resources based on the environment and the objectives. Our earlier examination of the nature of the environment suggests how problematic this can be for the strategist in light of linear, nonlinear, and stochastic behavior. Given the nature of the environment, "how" you seek to accomplish an objective will itself produce interaction within the environment. Part of the complexity is that an inappropriate instrument or a faulty application may well produce undesired second- and third-order effects. It is entirely possible to achieve a specified strategic objective but have the positive results sought subverted in the long run by the negative effect of the methods used. For example, the German military strategy in 1914 required that France be defeated rapidly first in order to preclude a prolonged two-front war. In order to accomplish the defeat of France, the German army's strategic concept called for the army to invade through Belgium. However, Belgium's neutrality was guaranteed by treaty, and the British leadership honored its commitment. Implementation of the German strategic concept thus led to Great Britain's entry into the war, which in turn precluded a rapid defeat of France and eventually led to the entry of the United States. The United States provided the resources to defeat Germany.

The strategic appraisal and the identification of strategic factors serve the development and consideration of concepts. Because the appraisal identifies what is important relative to the interests, concepts may be derived from or suggested by factors and relationships among them, or precluded by a concept's adverse impact on specific factors. Hence, the strategist actively seeks and considers diverse and multiple concepts for the achievement of strategy's objectives. A thorough examination of multiple strategic concepts allows the strategist to avoid concepts entailing the most egregious undesirable second- and third-order effects, or to develop appropriate ways to mitigate them. It allows for the selection of the concept that best meets the criteria of suitability, acceptability, and feasibility. Examination of all strategic concepts has the additional advantage of allowing the strategist to consider flexibility and adaptability in the determination of the best concept. Moreover, if a concept employed is not successful, the effort devoted to considering multiple approaches facilitates adaptation or allows for the quicker shift to a new concept—so that national efforts can be more rapidly redirected toward accomplishment of the objective. Good strategy formulation purposely explores multiple and diverse concepts.

One area of particular confusion associated with concepts results from the hierarchical nature of strategy. The concept for a higher strategy often states or implies objectives for subordinate levels of strategy or planning as part of the "how" of the concept for achieving a strategic objective. Strategists or others often want to elevate these to an objective for the higher strategy. Such elevation is inappropriate as discussed earlier. It appears to add precision but actually detracts from the focus of what is most important to achieve. A simple test for distinguishing whether such an objective is part of the concept is to ask "in order to do what?" The answer to this question should lead directly back to the appropriate strategic objective. What you need to accomplish as an end when you ask this question is the real strategic objective. At the same time a higher-level objective may transfer directly to the lower level or the higher strategic concept may establish objectives for lower levels. Both the higher-level objective and concept may create implied objectives for the lower levels. In a hierarchical strategic system, higher strategy dictates to lower levels of strategy and planning through its objectives, concepts, and resources; lower levels inform higher but are subordinate to higher strategy.

Another alluring trap for the strategist and leadership is strategic monism; the belief that one strategic concept fits all situations.[5] History is replete with overzealous advocates of such strategic singularity. Usually the appeal appears to lie in its directness, application of technology, and appearance of efficiency—quicker, fewer tactical complications, and cheaper. Nuclear deterrence was a strategic concept initially embraced by the United States following World War II in large part as a substitute for conventional forces. Yet, when conflicts emerged, such as the Korean War, use of nuclear weapons was barred by policy considerations and practicality, and conventional military forces were required—a failure of the earlier policymakers and strategists to perceive the environment as it really existed. The initial strategic monism of nuclear deterrence left the United States without an appropriate military instrument to support policy short of nuclear war until the adoption by the Kennedy administration of a strategy of flexible response.[6] The precision strike argument, a modern version of strategic bombing, is a potential contemporary military example of strategic monism. It substitutes technology for manpower, reduces casualties, and seeks to force the adversary to concede with limited collateral damage. It is a powerful capability, and may be an essential one, but it is not a singular solution to military strategy. Technology does not change the essence of war, or even the cruel face of it in all circumstances. Technology is an enabler at the strategic level, not a substitute for a strategic concept.[7] But technology often outruns political and strategic maturity, creating strategic conditions or consequences that neither are prepared to deal with appropriately.[8] The national security professional must avoid the appeal of strategic monism.

Strategic monism can occur on a grander scale. Strategic flexibility and adaptability at the highest levels is relative to the ability of the state to bring to bear the whole range of the capabilities inherent to its elements of power. A State Department that is inadequately resourced limits the application of diplomatic instruments. An inadequately funded military would create a similar problem. On the other hand, if all the state has is a strong military, every strategic issue begins to look like a nail calling for the application of the military hammer. Expediency can also instigate a siren's call for the use of an existing capability. Policymakers and strategists at the highest levels must recognize the value of flexibility and, as a part of a grand strategy, determine what instruments to maintain and at what levels.

Another disastrous tendency in concept development is to elevate an operational concept to the strategic level. German blitzkrieg in World War II offers a classic example. Blitzkrieg sought to capitalize on the combined technology of armor and air power to create a modern "*Kesselschlacte*," in effect a strategic envelopment of the French army to force France's capitulation. While this operational concept enjoyed initial success and indeed had significant strategic consequences for those nations overrun, as a strategic concept it did not have the ability to achieve Germany's strategic objectives or create the strategic effects that Hitler sought at the national level. In the long run, it neither brought an end to the war in the west nor isolated England. It did not create the conditions to achieve *lebenraum* or result in a better end-state for Germany. It was rapidly negated by the Allied selection of strategic objectives and concepts that united multiple nations in opposition and defeated Germany by total mobilization and a multifront war. Hitler's over reliance on military operational superiority proved misplaced as the Allies developed countermeasures and brought superior forces to bear. In a similar manner, one could argue that the much-hyped "shock and awe" in Operation Iraqi Freedom was elevated from an operational concept to a strategic one in the minds of some strategists and planners. In such a misconception, the operational concept does not have the sophistication or comprehensiveness to achieve and sustain the strategic objectives, and invariably produces contrary effects in the strategic environment. Good operational concepts are crucial in support of strategy, but are subordinate to the strategic concept and are part of operational art.

The logic of strategy argues that the strategic concept answers the big question of "how" the objectives will be achieved by articulating clearly for subordinate levels who does what, when, where, how, and why in such a manner that the subordinate strategist or planner can see with clarity how the execution of the concept leads to the accomplishment of the objective and what he is required to do in order to support the strategy. It confines the subordinate strategy or planning to the strategic objectives and the relevant aspects of the strategic environment without unduly limiting the subordinate's creativity or prerogatives.

RESOURCES IN STRATEGY

Resources (means) in strategy formulation determine the types and levels of resources that are necessary to support the concepts of the strategy. In strategy, resources can be tangible or intangible. Examples of tangible resources include forces, people, equipment, money, and facilities. The primary issue with tangible resources is that they are seldom sufficient to support the best concept optimally. This shortage can be an actual inability to resource, the result of the desire on the part of leadership to be prudent and efficient with government funding, or competing demands. Intangible resources include things like culture, national will, international goodwill, courage, intellect, or even fanaticism. Intangible resources are problematic for the strategist in that they often are not measurable or are volatile. National will in a democracy is certainly an essential resource, particularly in a long-term strategy, but the issue for the strategist is that it is more apt to need engendering and sustainment than be a given and reliable. Hence, intangible resources should always be suspect. They require close examination to determine if they are not actually improperly expressed concepts or objectives. The responsibility of the strategist is to ensure that the resources necessary for the accomplishment of the objectives as envisioned by the concepts are articulated and available, and to be alert to the possibility of both tangible and intangible resources that can be used in creative and innovative ways.

The hierarchy and logic of strategy also function in consideration of resources. Resources increasingly are defined in detail as the planning level is approached. A national security or grand strategy could list "military forces" as a resource for its concepts, even if the appropriate-type forces did not exist, and still be consistent as long as the development of the forces was funded and the concept allowed the time for building the force. It would then be the responsibility of the subordinate level of strategy to develop an objective and concept for creating the force—moving from the general to the particular. Assignment of resources requires no verb. It merely expresses what is to be made available for use in applying the concepts to accomplish the objectives. Thus "to develop, build or establish a larger force" is a way; the "force" itself, or the dollars to build it, is the resource. In articulating strategy, using the discussion of means to describe concepts should be avoided, as should articulating concepts as resources. In a very simplified manner, "diplomacy" is a strategic concept, but diplomats are among the resources required for the use of diplomacy. Imprecision in the vocabulary and logic of strategy leads to confusion and encourages friction at lower levels. The student of *On War* knows Clausewitz preferred "overthrow of the enemy's government" as the end, "to fight a decisive battle" as the way, and "a large army" as the means. He saw the large army as an appropriate resource to support his way—the decisive battle. But saying *to use* a large army" implies a range of different concepts for success. The employment of verbs to describe resources frequently suggests a problem within the logic of the strategy.

The rule of thumb to apply is that resources can usually be quantified, if only in general terms: State Department personnel, embassies, the Army, the Air Force, the Navy, units, and armed forces of United States; DoD personnel; dollars; facilities; equipment—trucks, planes, ships, etc.; and resources of organizations—Red Cross, North Atlantic Treaty Organization (NATO), etc. The strategist should state these as resources in terms that make clear to subordinate levels what is to be made available to support the concepts. How the resources are to be used is articulated in the concept. The specific development of resources is refined in the subordinate strategy and planning processes.

Resource selection, like concepts, has implications in regard to multilevel effects. Military resources can do a lot of things—fight wars, humanitarian operations, and nation-building are examples. While military forces may be the only available resources, the choice may have consequences. Military forces providing tsunami relief may not be as effective as experienced civilian nongovernmental agencies or may be perceived as a threat to the sovereignty of the supported nations. Military forces involved in nation building may be perceived by some as an occupying force, thus becoming the problem as opposed to part of the solution. If policy or circumstances dictate the use of the resources in such circumstances, the strategist's responsibility is to be aware of the potential second- and third-order effects and to consider such effects in the development of the strategy.

Resources are an integral part of good strategy. And while efficiency can be gained in the aggregate by doing things better, resources are usually the primary focus of efficiency advocates who often promote doing the same things with less. Allocating inadequate resources for a strategic concept is a recipe for disaster, and will cause even greater costs in recovering. Another commonly heard refrain among the military profession at large, and others, is that resources drive strategy. There is an element of truth in this statement. Resources are almost always limited at the strategic level because of competing demands from diverse needs. The strategist's responsibility is to ensure that the strategic concept will accomplish the objective, and that it is resourced to do so. A better concept may require less or different resources. A strategy that is not adequately or is inappropriately resourced is not a viable strategy at all.

TESTING STRATEGY'S VALIDITY AND RISK

All strategy has its own inherent logic, which can be assessed to determine validity and risk. The identification of resources in the development process is a good starting point for testing a strategy's internal logic. The strategist should think backward through the process to ensure the resources provided are adequate to implement the concepts, that the concepts envisioned can achieve the stated objectives in an acceptable manner, that the accomplishment of the objectives will create the strategic effects to satisfy the policy aims and promote and protect the national interests, and so forth. Thus, the strategist questions suitability—will the strategy's attainment accomplish the effect desired; he questions feasibility—can the action be accomplished by the means available; and he questions acceptability—are the effects as well as the methods and resources used to achieve those effects justified and acceptable to the body politic? In this process, the strategist considers tangibles, such as resource availability, weapons capability, and geography, and intangibles, such as national will, public opinion, world opinion, and actions/reactions of U.S. allies, adversaries, and other nations and actors. A strategy that can clearly be labeled as unsuitable, infeasible, or unacceptable is not valid. However, if an appropriate strategy formulation process has been adhered to, this will rarely be the case and the strategy is likely to be assessed as valid with qualifications—the qualifications being the measure of risk.

Risk is an assessment of the balance among what is known, assumed and unknown, as well as the correspondence between what is to be achieved and the concepts envisioned, and resources available. Risk assessment is not just a measure of the probability of success *or* failure. It is also an assessment of the probable consequences of success *and* failure. The strategic environment responds as a complex system—acting successfully, acting unsuccessfully, and failing to act must be anticipated and weighed. Since there are seldom enough resources or a clever enough concept to guarantee absolute success, there is always some risk in a dynamic strategic environment. Complexity, friction, and the freedom of choice of other actors also guarantee some element of risk. Risk weighs the potential advantages and disadvantages of adopting the strategy.

Risk assessment examines the strategy in its entire logic—ends, ways, and means—in the context of the environment and seeks to determine what effects are created by the implementation of the strategy. It seeks to determine how the equilibrium is affected and whether the environment is more or less favorable for the state as a result of the strategy. It asks how other actors will react to what has been attempted or achieved; how they will react to the way in which the strategy was pursued; what the balance is between intended and unintended consequences; what are these unintended consequences and what are the costs to recover from them; and how chance or friction will play in this strategy. The strategist must assess how the assumptions made or factors that might change could impact on success or effects. He must ask how much flexibility is inherent to the strategy, how it can be changed or recovered, and at what cost; what are the factors in the strategic environment the strategy is relying on for success; and what are the consequences if these change and is the strategy flexible or adaptable enough to accommodate these changes? It should be evident that the strategic appraisal and the determination of the strategic factors lay the foundation for this assessment. Risk assessment is an integral part of the strategy formulation process and should lead to acceptance, modification, or rejection of the strategy.

The strategist seeks to minimize risk through his development of the strategy—the relationship or balance of ends, ways, and means. But ultimately the strategist informs the decision makers of the risks in the strategy so the leaders can decide if the risks are acceptable or not. In a similar manner, strategic thinking guides the consideration of risk in policy formulation.

MONITOR FOR SUCCESS, FAILURE, OR MODIFICATION

The final step in the strategy formulation process is one of continuous monitoring or review of the strategy as it is being implemented. Continuous assessment should be a formalized, recurring process during the life of the strategy that evaluates the strategy's ends, ways, means, and risks against the evolving realities and possibilities in the strategic environment. The assessment evaluates for success, failure, essential modifications, or continued appropriateness in regard to the realization of the designated end-state(s). The strategic environment is dynamic and continuous change is inherent to it. Strategies that are successful may present new opportunities or require a new strategy to account for the conditions of success. Strategies that are failing beg for replacement. In addition, unforeseen changes in the strategic environment may occur that justify modification of some aspects of an existing strategy, but are not significant enough to invalidate the greater whole of the strategy. Lastly, national interests and policy could also change over time and as a result new strategies or modifications to existing strategies may be appropriate. Ideally, properly formulated strategy is constructed with inherent flexibility and adaptability in its statements of ends, ways, and means. Continuous changes beyond the requirements of success, failure, and changed conditions beyond the control of the formulators of the strategy, may be an indicator of poor strategic thinking or a flawed strategy formulation process. Nonetheless, both the strategic environment and the strategy are continuously assessed to ensure strategy supports the directing policy and interests appropriately.

CONCLUSION

Theory and practice provide insights into how to develop and articulate the ends, ways, and means of strategy, and the relationships among them. However, formulation of any strategy is the product of deep and iterative thinking. It is founded in a proper strategic appraisal and its ends, ways, means, and risks are assessed against a comprehensive and synergistic understanding of the strategic factors yielded by the appraisal. Strategy must be communicated clearly and carefully in its ends, ways, means, and justification of why because the communication affects what subordinates understand and will try to implement; the national will and its sustainability; and how others in the international community will act and react in regard to the strategy. The internal logic of strategy is tested through the criteria of feasibility, acceptability, and suitability. Strategy that does not meet these criteria is not a valid strategy, but even valid strategy has risk inherent to it. The strategist mitigates risk where he can, but ultimately can only inform the decision maker of the nature of the risk and the potential advantages and disadvantages of pursuing or not pursuing the strategy. The strategic thought processes involved in the formulation of strategy are equally valid for national security professionals responsible for working policy issues, formulating policy, and evaluating or implementing policy and strategy.

10

Strategy's Paradigm: Theory and Process Restated

> ... strategy has a complex nature and a function that is unchanging over the centuries.[1]
>
> —Colin S. Gray

At the highest level of strategy, the nation-state has interests that it pursues to the best of its abilities through the use of the instruments of power. Policy articulates the reflection of these interests in the strategic environment. In pursuing its policies, the state confronts adversaries and other actors, while some factors simply remain beyond control or unforeseen. Strategy, acting within the confines of theory, is a method of creating strategic effects favorable to policy and interests by applying ends, ways, and means in the strategic environment. In doing this, strategy has an inherent logic that can be understood as a theoretical construct and applied in the development and consideration of strategy at all levels.

Strategy applies in the realm of the strategic environment, which is characterized by greater or less degrees of chaotic behavior and complexity—VUCA (volatility, uncertainty, complexity, and ambiguity). The environment can be addressed at different levels of strategy. It has an inherent internal–external dialectic—a duality that produces successive interaction and results in multiordered effects. The international environment and the domestic environment are representative of this dialectic. Rational and irrational choice, chance and probability, competitors, allies, other actors, technology, geography, and nature are all part of the strategic paradigm.

Strategy is fundamentally a choice; it reflects a preference for a future state or condition in the strategic environment. It assumes that, while the future cannot be predicted, the strategic environment can be studied and assessed. Through the use of the strategic appraisal trends, issues, opportunities, threats, and other factors can be identified and, with the exception of chance, influenced and shaped through what the state chooses to do or not do. Thus, strategy seeks to influence and shape the future environment as opposed to simply reacting to it. Strategy at the state level can be defined as:

> The art and science of developing and using the political, economic, socio psychological and military power of the state to create strategic effects that protect or advance national interests in the environment in accordance with policy guidance. Strategy seeks a synergy and symmetry of objectives, concepts, and resources to increase the probabilities and favorable consequences of policy success and to lessen the chances of policy failure.

PREMISES OF STRATEGY

1. Strategy is proactive and anticipatory, but not predictive. Strategy seeks to promote or protect national interests as the future unfolds. In doing this it must consider change and make assumptions. Both change and assumptions are bounded by existing facts and realistic possibilities. Strategy is clear on what are facts, assumptions, and possibilities.

2. Strategy is subordinate to policy. Political purpose dominates all levels of strategy. Policy ensures that strategy pursues appropriate aims in an acceptable manner. However, the development of strategy informs policy; policy must adapt itself to the realities of the environment and the limits of power. Thus, policy ensures that strategy pursues appropriate aims, and strategy informs policy of the art of the possible.

3. Strategy is contextual and subordinate to the nature of the environment. Strategy must identify an appropriate balance among the objectives sought, the methods to pursue the objectives, and the resources available in the context of the strategic situation and inherent nature of the strategic environment. Strategy must be consistent with the particular context and the strategic environment's nature.

4. Strategy maintains a holistic perspective. It demands comprehensive consideration. Strategy is developed from a thorough consideration of the strategic situation and knowledge of the nature of the strategic environment. Strategic assessment highlights the internal and external factors in the strategic environment that help define strategic effect and the specific objectives, concepts, and resources of the strategy. Strategy reflects a comprehensive knowledge of what else is happening within the strategic environment and the potential multiorder effects of its own

choices on the efforts of those above, below, and on the strategist's own level.

5. Strategy creates a security dilemma for the strategist and other actors. Any strategy, once known or implemented, threatens the status quo and creates risk for the equilibrium of the strategic environment.[2] The strategist must determine if the end-state justifies the risks of initiating action, and other actors must decide if to act and in what manner.

6. Strategy is founded in what is to be accomplished and why it is to be accomplished. Strategy focuses on a preferred end-state among possible end-states in a dynamic environment. It provides direction for the coercive or persuasive use of the instruments of power to achieve specified objectives, thereby creating strategic effects leading to the desired end-state. The strategist must comprehend the nature of the strategic environment, the policy, and the nation's aggregate interests to determine what strategic effect is necessary before proper objectives can be determined.

7. Strategy is an inherently human enterprise. It is more than an intellectual consideration of objective factors. The role of belief systems and cultural perceptions of all the actors is important in strategy's formulation and implementation.

8. Friction is an inherent part of strategy. Friction is the summation of all the differences in how strategy is supposed to work versus how it actually unfolds when implemented. Friction cannot be eliminated, but it can be anticipated and accounted for to a greater or lesser extent by the formulation of good strategy.

9. Strategy focuses on root purposes and causes. This focus makes strategy inherently adaptable and flexible. Strategy learns from experience and must be sufficiently broad and flexible in its construction to adapt to unfolding events and an adversary's countermoves. Strategy's focus on root causes and purposes ensures that direction of subordinate levels is sufficiently broad to be adaptable and flexible.

10. Strategy is hierarchical. Just as strategy is subordinate to policy, lower levels of strategy and planning are subordinate to higher levels of strategy. The hierarchical nature of strategy facilitates span of control.

11. Strategy exists in a symbiotic relationship with time. Strategy must be integrated into the stream of history; it must be congruous with what has already happened and with the realistic possibilities of the future. Small changes at the right time can have large and unexpected consequences. Consequently, an intervention at an early date has greater effect at less cost than a later intervention. Strategy is about thinking and acting in time in a way that is fundamentally different than planning.

12. Strategy is cumulative. Effects in the strategic environment are cumulative; once given birth, they become a part of the play of continuity and change. Strategies at different levels interact and influence the success of higher and lower strategy and planning over time.

13. Efficiency is subordinate to effectiveness in strategy. Strategic objectives, if accomplished, create or contribute to strategic effects that lead to the achievement of the desired end-state at the level of strategy being analyzed. In that way, they ultimately serve national interests. Good strategy is both effective and efficient, but effectiveness takes precedence over efficiency. Concepts and resources serve objectives without undue risk of failure or unintended effects.

14. Strategy provides a proper relationship or balance among the objectives sought, the methods to pursue the objectives, and the resources available. In formulating a strategy, the ends, ways, and means are part of an integral whole and work synergistically to achieve strategic effect at that level of strategy, as well as contribute to cumulative effects at higher levels. Ends, ways, and means must be in concert qualitatively and quantitatively, both internally and externally. From the synergistic balance of ends, ways, and means the strategy achieves suitability, acceptability, and feasibility.

15. Risk is inherent to all strategy. Strategy is subordinate to the uncertain nature of the strategic environment. Success is contingent on implementation of an *effective* strategy—ends, ways, and means that positively interact with the strategic environment. Failure is the inability to achieve one's objectives, the thwarting of achievement of one's objectives by other actors or chance, the creation of unintended adverse effects of such magnitude as to negate what would otherwise be regarded as strategic success, or the consequences of not acting. Risk assessment is not just the measure of the probabilities of *success or failure*, but an assessment of all the probable consequences of *success and failure*.

THE STRATEGIC APPRAISAL PROCESS

The purpose of the strategic appraisal process is to clarify and express interests with specificity; determine the intensity of interests; evaluate information, assumptions, and inferences to identify what is important to those interests; determine all strategic factors; and choose key strategic factors on which to base a strategy. This appraisal along with the strategist's weltanschauung also provides the basis for ensuring strategy's feasibility, acceptability, and suitability and the basis for assessing risk. In addition, in the implementation of strategy, the continuous assessment and any necessary adaptation or replacement of strategy are served by the knowledge gained in the strategic appraisal.

1. *Stimulus or Requirement.* A stimulus such as a major environmental change, new national policy, or requirement to update strategy demands the conduct of a new strategic appraisal. This appraisal is tailored to the

realm of the strategy pursued in both kind and level, but it is holistic in its outlook.

2. *Determine and Articulate Interests.* Interests are expressed as statements of desired end-states or conditions and do not imply intended actions or set objectives—policy and strategy does this. Consequently, interests are stated without verbs or other action modifiers. Interests should be expressed with an appropriate degree of specificity. Specificity in interests serves the multiple purposes of clarifying policy's intent in different strategy realms, focusing attention on the appropriate strategic factors, and reinforcing proper strategy formulation—establishing responsibility, authority, and accountability.

3. *Determine Intensity of Interests.* Levels of intensity suggest relative importance and have temporal, resource, and risk acceptance implications, but the decision to act or how to act in regard to them flows from the whole of the strategy formulation process—not the assignment of the intensity. Intensity levels are transitory in that they are subject to change based on the perception of urgency associated with them at any time. Intensity is dependent on the context of the strategic situation and the policymaker or strategist's interpretation of the context and the importance of the interest to national well-being. Levels of intensity include:

Survival—If unfulfilled, will result in immediate massive destruction of one or more major aspects of core interests.

Vital—If unfulfilled, will have immediate consequence for core national interests.

Important—If unfulfilled, will result in damage that will eventually affect core national interests.

Peripheral—If unfulfilled, will result in damage that is unlikely to affect core national interests.[3]

4. *Assess Information.* The strategist casts a wide net to bring together and assess the information relative to the interests. Information includes facts and data relating to any aspect of the strategic environment in regard to the interest(s), including: both tangible and intangible attributes and knowledge, assumptions, relationships, and interaction. All information is assessed from friendly, neutral, and adversarial perspectives and from objective and subjective perspectives in each case. While emphasis is logically on the realm of strategy being formulated, holistic thinking is applied to look both vertically and horizontally at other realms and across the environment.

From this assessment the strategist will identify and evaluate the strategic factors that affect or potentially affect the interests—whether promoting, hindering, protecting, or threatening them. From his evaluation of the factors, he will select the key strategic factors—the factors on which his strategy will be based.

5. *Determine Strategic Factors.* Strategic factors are the things that can potentially contribute or detract causally to the realization of the interest. Factors may be tangible or intangible, representing any aspect of the environment. The existence of other states and actors, geography, culture, history, relationships, perspectives and perceptions, facts, and assumptions all represent potential factors. What the strategist understands they are and what others believe them to be are both important.

6. *Select Key Factors.* Key strategic factors are those strategic factors at the crux of strategic interaction, representing the potential critical points of tension between continuities and change within the environment. Using, influencing, and countering them is how the strategist pursues, advances, or protects interests. Strategy seeks to change, leverage, or overcome these, in effect modifying or retaining the equilibrium within the strategic environment by setting objectives and developing concepts, and marshaling resources to achieve the objectives. When successfully selected and achieved, the objectives create strategic effects that tip the balance in favor of the stated interests. The selection of key factors is a choice made by the strategist based on the appraisal. Key factors may work individually or synergistically with one another, but none should lead to strategy that is internally contradictive.

7. *Formulate Strategy.* The strategist's assessment of how to best interact with the key strategic factors is reflected in his calculation of the relationship of ends, ways, and means—the rationally stated output of strategic thought. The calculation and each of its components are based on the strategist's assessment of the relationships among the desired end-state and various key factors as well as the interdependence among all the other factors.

STRATEGY FORMULATION (ENDS, WAYS, AND MEANS)

Strategy is expressed in terms of ends, ways, and means. Ends, ways, and means that lead to the achievement of the desired end-state within acceptable bounds of feasibility, suitability, acceptability, and risk are valid strategies for consideration by the decision maker.

Objectives (ends) explain "what" is to be accomplished. They flow from a consideration of the interests and the factors in the strategic environment affecting the achievement of the desired end-state. Objectives are bounded by policy guidance, higher strategy, the nature of the strategic environment, the capabilities and limitations of the instruments of powers of the state, and resources made available. Objectives are selected to create strategic effect. Strategic objectives, if accomplished, create or contribute to strategic effects that lead to the achievement of the desired end-state at the level of strategy being analyzed and, ultimately, serve national interests. In strategy objectives are expressed with explicit verbs (e.g., deter war, promote regional stability, destroy Iraqi armed forces). Explicit verbs force the strategist to consider and qualify what is to be accomplished and help establish the parameters for the use of power.

Strategic concepts (ways) explain the big question of "how" the objectives are to be accomplished by the employment of the instruments of power. They link resources to the objectives by addressing who does what, where, when, how, and why, with the answers to which explaining "how" an objective will be achieved. Since concepts convey action, they often employ verbs in their construction, but are actually descriptions of "how" the objective of a strategy is to be accomplished. Strategic concepts provide direction and boundaries for subordinate strategies and planning. A strategic concept must be explicit enough to provide planning guidance to those identified to implement and resource it, but not so detailed as to eliminate creativity and initiative at subordinate strategy and planning levels. Logically, concepts become more specific at lower levels.

Resources (means) in strategy formulation set the boundaries for the types and levels of support modalities that will be made available for pursuing concepts of the strategy. In strategy, resources can be tangible or intangible. Examples of tangible means include forces, people, equipment, money, and facilities. Intangible resources include things like culture, will, courage, or intellect. Intangible resources are often problematic for the strategist in that they are often immeasurable or are volatile. Hence, intangible resources should always be suspect and closely examined to determine whether they are actually improperly expressed concepts or objectives. The rule of thumb to apply is that resources can usually be quantified, if only in general terms. The strategist states resources in terms that make clear to subordinate levels what is to be made available to support the concepts.

VALIDITY AND RISK

Strategy has an inherent logic of suitability, feasibility, and acceptability. These would naturally be considered as the strategy is developed, but the strategy should be validated against them once it has been fully articulated. Thus, the strategist questions

> Suitability—Will the attainment of the objectives using the instruments of power in the manner stated accomplish the strategic effects desired?
>
> Feasibility—Can the strategic concept be executed with the resources available?
>
> Acceptability—Do the strategic effects sought justify the objectives pursued, the methods used to achieve them, and the costs in blood, treasure, and potential insecurity for the domestic and international communities? In this process, one considers intangibles such as national will, public opinion, world opinion, and actions/reactions of U.S. allies, adversaries, and other nations and actors.

The questions of suitability, feasibility, and acceptability as expressed above are really questions about the validity of the strategy, not the risk. If the answer to any of the three questions is "no," the strategy is not valid. But strategy is not a black and white world, and the strategist may find that the answer to one or more of these questions is somewhat ambiguous.

Risk is determined through the assessment of the probable consequences of success and failure. It examines the strategy in its entire logic—ends, ways, and means—in the context of the strategic environment, and seeks to determine what strategic effects are created by the strategy's implementation. It seeks to determine how the equilibrium is affected and whether the strategic environment is more or less favorable for the state as a result of the strategy. Risk is clarified by asking the following questions:

What assumptions were made in this strategy, and what is the effect, if any, of them is wrong?

What internal or external factors were considered in the development of the strategy? What change in regard to these factors would positively or adversely affect the success or effects of the strategy?

What flexibility or adaptability is inherent to the components of the strategy? How can the strategy be modified and at what cost?

How will other actors react to what has been attempted or achieved? How will they react to the way in which the strategy was pursued?

What is the balance between intended and unintended consequences? What are the possible unintended consequences and what are the costs to recover from them?

How will chance or friction play in this strategy?

11

Concluding Thoughts

> Good strategy does not recognize the concept of victory. There are no victories; there are only phase lines in a permanent struggle to promote and define our national interests.[1]
>
> —Gary L. Guertner

Good policy and strategy formulation require the national security professional to step out of the planning mind-set and adopt one more suited for strategic thinking. In the strategic mind-set, the strategist and others embrace the complexity and chaos of the strategic environment and envision all its continuities and possibilities in seeking to create favorable strategic effects in support of the national interests. From an accurate assessment of the strategic environment, the strategist or policymaker determines the threats to and opportunities for the advancement or protection of these interests. Supported by formal and informal policy formulation structure, the policymaker applies his strategic thinking and political skills in the inherently political process of negotiating and articulating national policy. From policy, the strategist receives the political leadership's vision, guidance, and priorities of effort in regard to interests. Thus, in constructing a valid strategy, the strategist is bounded by the nature of the strategic environment, the dictates of policy, and the logic of strategy. The strategist is responsible for mastering the external and internal facets of the strategic environment, adhering to policy or seeking change, and applying the logic of strategy-to-strategy formulation in a disciplined manner. He articulates the strategy in the rational model of ends, ways, and means; but leadership remains responsible for the decision to adopt the strategy.

Good strategy demands much of the strategist as good policy demands much of the policymaker. The strategist or national security professional must be a constant student of the strategic environment as reflected externally and internally. He must be immersed in the events of today while aware of the legacies of the past and the possibilities of the future. His weltanschauung is both an objective view of the current strategic environment and an anticipatory appreciation of what can be. In one sense, the strategist uses the strategic appraisal to sort through an arena of cognitive dissonance to the "real" truth—what is really important. The real truth best serves interests and policy in the long run; the strategist must reject the expedient, near-term solution for the long-term benefit. The strategist intervenes through action or selected non-action to create a more favorable strategic environment. In this process, everything has meaning, and everything has potential consequences. The strategist cannot be omniscient, but the strategist can be open and aware—open to the possibilities and aware of the consequences. If the strategist is sufficiently open and aware, he can anticipate the future and formulate successful strategy. If in practice the strategist is not immersed in uncertainty and ambiguity and examining the context of the past, the emerging events of today, and the possibilities of tomorrow, he is probably not doing strategy—but rather planning under the label of strategy. Thus, the proper focus of policy and strategy is to clarify and exert influence over the strategic environment in order to create strategic effects favorable to the interests of the state. This is done by articulation of ends, ways, and means that create the desired strategic effect.

Policy and strategy are neither simple nor easy. Nothing in this book should suggest either. Strategic thinking is difficult because it deals with the incredible complexity and unpredictability of the strategic environment. Its essence is to simplify this volatility, uncertainty, complexity, and ambiguity—the VUCA—in a rational expression of ends, ways, and means so that planners can create a degree of certainty and a more predictable outcome. In this regard, it bounds planning but does not unnecessarily restrict the planner. Nor should anything in this text suggest that strategy is vague or imprecise. The complex and ambiguous must be reduced and made clear without loss of understanding of the comprehensiveness of interaction within the strategic environment. Strategy seeks great clarity and precision in developing and articulating objectives and concepts—but it does this in a manner appropriate to the strategic level. The logic of strategy requires that these be expressed in terms that allow for flexibility and adaptation; thus do not unnecessarily confine innovation and initiative at subordinate levels. This requirement reinforces the need for clarity of thought and word so that strategic purpose and direction are evident.

Relative success is the product of good policy and strategy: relative to objectives, relative to "current" reality, relative to the future, relative to risk, relative to costs, and relative to adversaries and allies. Strategic thinking should be precise and clear in its articulation, but it is anticipatory—not predictive. The future changes as it unfolds because the strategic environment is dynamic. Core interests remain over time, but their expression in regard to specific strategic circumstances changes with time and context. Once implemented, policy and strategy by definition change the fundamental conditions and perspective generating it and is at risk in some part, if for no other reasons than chance and the freedom of choice of other actors. Thus, policy and strategy can be measured relatively against its objectives and the strategic effect they seek to produce, but it cannot guarantee the future. The future strategic environment is always the product of more than the sum of the parts of a given policy or strategy.

The theory of strategy teaches the national security professional "how to think" about policy and strategy, not "what to think" for either. It educates his mind and disciplines his thinking for the environment that confronts him as a policymaker, senior leader, strategist, or other national security professional so that he can serve the nation well. So armed, the politician or professional is prepared to formulate, evaluate, and implement policy and strategy appropriate for his place and time. Policy and strategy formulation and terminology are less pure in practice than in theory or as advocated herein. "Strategic planning" and other such "strategic labeling" are commonplace, and zealous advocates of various concepts and practices often seek to co-opt such terms to gain credibility and visibility. The serious minded should be neither seduced nor distracted by these manipulations but remain focused on strategic thinking proper—never confusing policy, strategy, and planning, and recognizing the validity and role of each. In this way, the politician, the professional, or the concerned citizen's contribution to the debate and to the formulation, evaluation, and implementation of policy or strategy will adhere to strategy's logic and his advice and recommendations will fully support desirable end-states.

And, finally, policy and strategy formulation is not the domain for the thin of skin or self-serving. Detractors stand ever ready to magnify a policy or strategy's errors or limitations. Even success is open to criticism from pundits who question policy or strategy's role, methods, or continued validity. Ultimately policy is rewarded or punished in the electoral process. Strategy is judged by its internal logic and the quality of its consequences. Furthermore, both achieve strategic consequences by the multiorder effects they create over time—always a point of contention in a time-conscience society that values immediate results and lacks patience with the "long view." In the end, it is the destined role of both the strategist and national security professional in general to be underappreciated and often demeaned in his own time. Consequently, the pursuit of national security and strategy remains the proper domain of the strong intellect, the life-long student, the dedicated professional, and the impervious ego—one which is well prepared and willing to wait for history to render judgment in regard to success.

Notes

CHAPTER 1

1. Williamson Murray and Mark Grimsley, "Introduction: On Strategy," in *The Making of Strategy: Rulers, States, and War* (Cambridge: Cambridge University Press, 1994; 1997) 22.

2. Peter F. Drucker, "The Global Economy and the Nation-State," *Foreign Affairs* 76(5) (September/October 1997). The author makes the defensive case even economic interdependence cannot overcome nationalism.

3. For a clear, concise argument for the issues confronting the United States in regard to a new twenty-first-century world order, see Henry Kissinger, *Diplomacy* (New York: Simon & Schuster, 1994) 804–836.

4. Joint Staff, J-7, *Joint Publication 1-02, Department of Defense Dictionary of Military and Associated Terms* (Washington, DC: United States Joint Staff, April 12, 2002; amended through September 14, 2007) 518.

5. Sun-tzu, *The Art of War*, trans. Ralph D. Sawyer (New York: Barnes & Noble Books, 1994); Carl von Clausewitz, *On War*, ed. and trans. Michael Howard and Peter Paret (Princeton: Princeton University Press, 1976); Colin S. Gray, *Modern Strategy* (Oxford: Oxford University Press, 1999).

6. Gregory D. Foster, "A Conceptual Foundation for a Theory of Strategy," *The Washington Quarterly* (Winter 1990): 43. Foster's analysis of the assumptions and premises of strategy is particularly thought provoking.

7. Clausewitz, *On War*, 141.

8. Ibid., 100–102.

9. Gray, *Modern Strategy*, 33–34, 51–54.

CHAPTER 2

1. Carl von Clausewitz, *On War*, ed. and trans. Michael Howard and Peter Paret (Princeton: Princeton University Press, 1976) 177–178.

2. See Richard L. Kugler, *Policy Analysis in National Security Affairs* (Washington, DC: National Defense University Press, 2006) 12–16. In four pages Kugler catches the "Essence of Policy."

3. National Security Council, "NSC 68: United States Objectives and Programs for National Security (April 14, 1950): A Report to the President Pursuant to the President's Directive of January 31, 1950," Washington, DC (April 7, 1950), available from http://www.fas.org/irp/offdocs/nsc-hst/nsc-68.htm: Internet accessed September 29, 2007.

4. Richard M. Meinhart, "Leadership and Strategic Thinking," in *Strategic Thinking* (Carlisle, PA: U.S. Army War College, 2007). USAWC teaches a model that highlights five strategic thinking competencies, all of which are applied in the strategy formulation process. These and other competencies apply in the avocation and execution of the strategy.

5. Ibid.

6. Colonel Stephen J. Gerras, "Thinking Critically About Critical Thinking: A Fundamental Guide for Strategic Leaders," in *Strategic Thinking* (Carlisle, PA: U.S. Army War College, 2007) 47–75.

7. George E. Reed. "Systems Thinking and Senior Level Leadership" in *Strategic Thinking* (Carlisle, PA: U.S. Army War College, 2007) 158–162.

8. Col Charles D. Allen, "Creative Thinking for Individuals and Teams," in *Strategic Thinking* (Carlisle, PA: U.S. Army War College, 2007) 47–75.

9. Richard E. Neustadt and Ernest R. May, *Thinking in Time: The Use of History for Decision Makers* (New York: The Free Press, 1986) 252–256.

10. Meinhart, "Leadership and Strategic Thinking," 44.

11. Clausewitz, *On War*, 136–137.

12. Colin S. Gray, *Modern Strategy* (Oxford: Oxford University Press, 1999) 30–31, 49, 68–74, 97, 106–107.

13. MG Richard A. Chilcoat, *Strategic Art: The New Discipline for the 21st Century* (Carlisle, PA: Strategic Studies Institute, 1995) 6–9.

CHAPTER 3

1. Colin S. Gray, *Modern Strategy* (Oxford: Oxford University Press, 1999) 1.

2. David Jablonsky, *Why Is Strategy Difficult?* (Carlisle Barracks, PA: Strategic Studies Institute, U.S. Army War College, 1992; repr. 1995) 10.

3. Gregory D. Foster, "A Conceptual Foundation for a Theory of Strategy," *The Washington Quarterly* (Winter 1990): 47–48.

4. Carl von Clausewitz, *On War*, ed. and trans. Michael Howard and Peter Paret (Princeton: Princeton University Press, 1976) 89.

5. Foster, "A Conceptual Foundation for a Theory of Strategy," 50.

6. Arthur F. Lykke, Jr., "Toward an Understanding of Military Strategy," in *Military Strategy: Theory and Application* (Carlisle Barracks, PA: U.S. Army War College, 1989) 3–8.

7. Clausewitz, *On War*, 87.

8. Foster, "A Conceptual Foundation for a Theory of Strategy," 50.

9. Clausewitz, *On War*, 86–87, 607–608.

10. Robert Jervis, *System Effects: Complexity in Political and Social Life* (Princeton, NJ: Princeton University Press, 1997) 60.

11. Williamson Murray and Mark Grimsley, "Introduction: On Strategy," in *The Making of Strategy: Rulers, States, and War* (Cambridge: Cambridge University Press, 1994, 1997) 1, 13; Clausewitz, *On War*, 86, 89.

12. Stephen J. Cimbala, *Clausewitz and Chaos: Friction in War and Military Policy* (Westport, CT: Praeger, 2001) 7–14. While somewhat controversial, this book contributes important insights into the nature of the strategic environment.

13. Ibid., 8.

14. Murray and Grimsley, "Introduction: On Strategy," 1.

15. Department of National Security and Strategy, *Course 2 Course Directive AY 2005: "War, National Security Policy & Strategy* (Carlisle, PA: U.S. Army War College, 2004) 158.

16. Joint Staff, J-7, *Joint Publication 1-02, Department of Defense Dictionary of Military and Associated* Terms (Washington, DC: United States Joint Staff, April 12, 2002; amended through September 14, 2007) 360.

17. Ibid., 359.

18. Ibid., 535.

19. Donald H. Rumsfeld, Secretary of Defense, *The National Defense Strategy of The United States of America* (Washington, DC: Department of Defense, March 2005). Secretary Rumsfeld attempted to impose more civilian control over the military by eliminating the *National Military Strategy* developed by the Chairman of the Joint Chiefs of Staff but was reminded by Congress that it was required by law. *The National Defense Strategy* was placed in the hierarchy to make his point.

20. Foster, "A Conceptual Foundation for a Theory of Strategy," 56–57.

21. Murray and Grimsley, "Introduction: On Strategy," 6–7. See also Richard E. Neustadt and Ernest R. May, *Thinking in Time: The Use of History for Decision Makers* (New York: The Free Press, 1986) for practices and examples of how to do this.

22. Robert H. Dorff, "Strategy, Grand Strategy, and the Search for Security," in *The Search for Security: A U.S. Grand Strategy for the Twenty-First Century*, ed. Max G. Manwaring, Edwin G. Corr, and Robin H. Dorff (Westport, CT: Praeger, 2003) 128–129.

CHAPTER 4

1. Carl von Clausewitz, *On War*, ed. and trans. Michael Howard and Peter Paret (Princeton: Princeton University Press, 1976) 178.

2. William J. Doll, "Parsing the Future: A Frame of Reference to Scenario Building" (Unpublished Paper: Joint Warfare Analysis Center, 2005) 2–3.

3. Roderick R. Magee II, ed., *Strategic Leadership Primer* (Carlisle Barracks, PA: U.S. Army War College, 1998) 1.

4. Alvin M. Saperstein, "Complexity, Chaos, and National Security Policy: Metaphors or Tools" in *Complexity, Global Politics, and National Security*, ed.

David S. Alberts and Thomas J. Czerwinski, 1997, http://www.ndu.edu/inss/books/books%20-%201998/Complexity,%20Global%20Politics%20and%20Nat'l%20Sec%20-%20Sept%2098/ch05.html,accessed on December 8, 2004.

5. Alan D. Beyerchen, "Clausewitz, Nonlinearity, and the Importance of Imagery," in *Complexity, Global Politics, and National Security*, ed. David S. Alberts and Thomas J. Czerwinski, 1997, http://www.ndu.edu/inss/books/books%20-%201998/Complexity, %20Global%20Politics%20and%20Nat'l%20Sec%20-%20Sept%2098/ch07.html, accessed on December 8, 2004.

6. Manus J. Donahue III, "An Introduction to Mathematical Chaos Theory and Fractal Geometry," December 1997; available from http://www.fractalfinance.com/chaostheory.html; accessed on December 13, 2004.

7. Clausewitz, *On War*, 119.

8. Major Susan E. Durham, "Chaos Theory for the Practical Military Mind," March 1997; available from http://www.au.af.mil/au/awc/awcgate/acsc/97-0229.pdf; accessed on December 13, 2004. See also Donahue, "An Introduction to Mathematical Chaos Theory and Fractal Geometry."

9. Donahue, "An Introduction to Mathematical Chaos Theory and Fractal Geometry." See also John Lewis Gaddis, *The Landscape of History: How Historians Map the Past* (Oxford: Oxford University Press, 2002) 71–90.

10. Vicente Valle, Jr. "Chaos, Complexity and Deterrence," Student Paper at National War College, April 19, 2000; available from http://www.au.af.mil/au/awc/awcgate/ndu/valle.pdf, accessed on December 18, 2004, 4.

11. James N. Rosenau, "Damn Things Simultaneously: Complexity Theory and World Affairs," in *Complexity, Global Politics, and National Security*, ed. David S. Alberts and Thomas J. Czerwinski, 1997, http://www.ndu.edu/inss/books/books%20-%201998/Complexity,%20Global%20Politics%20and%20Nat'l%20Sec%20-%20Sept%2098/ch03.html, accessed on December 8, 2004.

12. Valle, "Chaos, Complexity and Deterrence," 2–3.

13. John F. Schmitt, "Command and (Out of) Control: The Military Implications of Complexity Theory," in *Complexity, Global Politics, and National Security*, ed. David S. Alberts and Thomas J. Czerwinski, 1997, http://www.ndu.edu/inss/books/books%20-%201998/Complexity,%20Global%20Politics%20and%20Nat'l%20Sec%20-%20Sept%2098/ch09.html, accessed on December 8, 2004.

14. Robert Jervis, "Complex Systems: The Role of Interactions," in *Complexity, Global Politics, and National Security*, ed. David S. Alberts and Thomas J. Czerwinski, 1997, http://www.ndu.edu/inss/books/books%20-%201998/Complexity,%20Global%20Politics%20and%20Nat'l%20Sec%20-%20Sept%2098/ch03.html, accessed on December 8, 2004.

15. Beyerchen, "Clausewitz, Nonlinearity, and the Importance of Imagery."

16. Any query into a research data base will substantiate this assertion and the subject is manifest in various sources ranging across a spectrum of interests: *The New York Times, Washington Quarterly, New Political Economy, Foreign Affairs, Parameters, The World Economy, Journal of Business Ethics, Third World Quarterly*, etc.

17. Michael J. Mazarr, "Theory and U.S. Military Strategy: A 'Leapfrog' Strategy for U.S. Defense Policy," in *Complexity, Global Politics, and National Security*, ed. David S. Alberts and Thomas J. Czerwinski, 1997, http://www.ndu.edu/inss/

books/books%20-%201998/Complexity,%20Global%20Politics%20and%
20Nat'l%20Sec%20-%20Sept%2098/ch11.html, accessed on December 23,
2004.

18. Ibid.

CHAPTER 5

1. Robert Cooper, *The Breaking of Nations: Order and Chaos in the 21st Century* (New York: Atlantic Monthly Press, 2003) 5.

2. Colin S. Gray, *Modern Strategy* (Oxford: Oxford University Press, 1999) 50.

3. Ibid., 23–43.

4. MacGregor Knox, "Conclusion: Continuity and Revolution in the Making of Strategy," in *The Making of Strategy: Rulers, States, and War* (Cambridge, UK: Cambridge University Press, 1994 [1997]) 615.

5. John Lewis Gaddis, *The Landscape of History: How Historians Map the Past* (Oxford: Oxford University Press, 2002) 61.

6. John Lewis Gaddis, "Grand Strategy in the Second Term," *Foreign Affairs* (January–February 2005): 14.

7. Robert Jervis, *System Effects: Complexity in Political and Social Life* (Princeton, NJ: Princeton University Press, 1997) 10–28, 60.

8. Knox, "Conclusion: Continuity and Revolution in the Making of Strategy," 643.

9. Shona L. Brown and Kathleen M. Eisenhardt, *Competing on the Edge: Strategy as Structured Chaos* (Boston, MA: Harvard Business School Press, 1998) 3–4, 7.

10. Gaddis, *The Landscape of History*, 56–57, 59.

11. Alan D. Beyerchen, "Clausewitz, Nonlinearity, and the Importance of Imagery," in *Complexity, Global Politics, and National Security*, ed. David S. Alberts and Thomas J. Czerwinski, 1997, http://www.ndu.edu/inss/books/books%20-%201998/Complexity, %20Global%20Politics%20and%20Nat'l%20Sec%20-%20Sept%2098/ch07.html, accessed on December 8, 2004.

12. Jack Synder, "One World Rival Theories," *Foreign Policy* (November–December 2004): 53–62.

13. Knox, "Conclusion: Continuity and Revolution in the Making of Strategy," 627.

14. James Kurth, "Inside the Cave: The Banality of I.R. Studies," *The National Interest* (Fall 1998): 38–40.

15. Knox, "Conclusion: Continuity and Revolution in the Making of Strategy," 645.

16. Gaddis, "Grand Strategy," 10.

17. Knox, "Conclusion: Continuity and Revolution in the Making of Strategy," 645.

18. Gaddis, *The Landscape of History*, 65.

19. Bart Kosko, *Fuzzy Thinking: The New Science of Fuzzy Logic* (New York: Hyperion, 1993) 4–22. The humanities are a noteworthy exception to this pervasiveness but even here quantification has been applied by some to seek the "right" explanation.

20. Carl von Clausewitz, *On War*, ed. and trans. Michael Howard and Peter Paret (Princeton: Princeton University Press, 1976) 120.

21. Ibid., 119.

22. Gaddis, *The Landscape of History*, 61, 64, 68–69.

23. Gray, *Modern Strategy*, 19–20.

CHAPTER 6

1. Carl von Clausewitz, *On War*, ed. and trans. Michael Howard and Peter Paret (Princeton: Princeton University Press, 1976) 605.

2. U.S. Department of State, *Treaties in Force*, 2 vols. Sections 1 and 2, Listing, available at http://www.state.gov/s/l/treaty/treaties/2007/index.htm, accessed on September 29, 2007.

3. John Spanier and Robert l. Wendzel, *Games Nations Play*, 9th ed. (Washington, DC: Congressional Quarterly, Inc., 1996).

4. Ibid., 11–13.

5. Ibid.

6. Ibid.

7. Ibid.

8. Ibid., 10–11. Graham Allison and Philip Zelikow, *Essence of Decision: Explaining the Cuban Missile Crisis*, 2nd ed. (New York: Addison-Wesley Educational Publishers Inc., 1999) 36–40.

9. E.H. Carr, *The Twenty Year's Crisis, 1919–1939: An Introduction to the Study of International Relations*, 2nd ed. (London: Macmillan and Company Ltd., 1956).

10. Ibid.

11. Ole R. Holst, "Theories of International Relation," in *Explaining the History of International Relations*, ed. Michael J. Hogan and Thomas G. Patterson, 2nd ed. (Cambridge, UK: Cambridge University Press, 2004) 60–61, 67–69.

12. Spanier and Wendzel, *Games Nations Play*, 119.

13. Ibid., 117–121.

14. Ibid., 119–124, 110–111.

15. Ibid.

16. Seyom Brown, *Multilateral Contraints on the Use of Force: A Reassessment* (Carlisle, PA: Strategic Studies Institute, March 2006) 4–14.

17. Spanier and Wendzel, *Games Nations Play*, 43–52.

18. Ibid.

19. 1 Bruce D. Porter, *War and the Rise of the State: Military Foundations of Modern Politics* (New York: The Free Press, 1994) 302. For another discussion of the issue and defense of the nation—state, see also Martin Wolf, "Will the Nation-State Survive Globalization?" *Foreign Affairs* 80(1) (January/February 2001): 178–190.

20. Spanier and Wendzel, *Games Nations Play*, 62.

21. Ibid., 66.

22. Ibid., 66–68.

23. Ibid., 68–69.

24. Peter Willets, "Transnational Actors and International Organizations in Global Politics," in *The Globalization of World Politics: An Introduction*

to International Relations, 3rd ed., ed. John Baylis and Steve Smith (New York: Oxford University Press, 2001) 435–439.

25. Ibid., 433–435.

26. Kimberley Thachuk, "Transnational Threats: Falling through the Cracks," *Low Intensity Conflict and Law Enforcement* 10(1) (Spring 2001): 50–51.

27. David Jablonsky, "National Power," in *U.S. Army War College Guide to National Security Policy and Strategy*, ed. J. Boone Bartholomees (Carlisle, PA: U.S. Army War College, June 2006) 127–142.

28. Spanier and Wendzel, *Games Nations Play*, 127–148. These authors argue that the presence of four factors are required for a power relationship to exist. This author rejects this. The relationship exists continuously, and in any interaction states will be aware of relative power.

29. Jablonsky, "National Power," 130–137. Jablonsky in this chapter actually separates socio-physiological into psychological and informational.

30. Ibid., 133–138.

31. A.T. Mahan, *The Influence of Sea Power Upon History 1660–1783* (New York: Dover Publications, Inc., reprint 1987) 1, 25–89.

32. Donald E. Nuechterlein, *America Overcommitted: United States National Interests in the 1980s* (Lexington, KY: The University Press of Kentucky, 1984) 31–53.

33. Commonly called the DIMEFIL Chart. It is used in Department of Defense to identify examples of the instruments of power, which are derived in this model from seven elements of power (Public Domain).

34. Thomas C. Schelling, *Arms and Influence* (New Haven, CT: Yale University Press, 1966) 1–18.

35. Ibid., 2–5.

36. Joseph S. Nye, *Soft Power: The Means to Success in World Politics* (New York: Public Affairs, 2004) 5–18, 25–32.

37. Edward C. Luck, "The United States, International Organizations, and the Quest for Legitimacy," in *Multilateralism and US Foreign Policy*, ed. Steward Patrick and Shepard Forman (Boulder, CO: Lynne Rienner Publishers, Inc., 2002) 47.

38. Ibid., 47–48.

39. Ibid., 40–42.

40. Thomas M. McShane, "International Law and the New World Order: Refining Sovereignty," in U.S. Army War College Guide to National Security Policy and Strategy, 2nd ed., ed. J. Boone Bartholomees, Jr. (Carlisle, PA: U.S. Army War College, June 2006) 43–46.

41. Robert Cooper, *The Breaking of Nations: Order and Chaos in the 21st Century* (New York: Atlantic Monthly Press, 2003) 149–151, 156–172.

42. Edward N. Luttwak, *Strategy: The Logic of War and Peace*, Rev. and Enlarged (Cambridge, MA: The Belknap Press, 1987, 2001) 3.

43. Andrew H. Kydd and Barbara F. Walter, "The Strategies of Terrorism," *International Security* 31(1) (Summer 2006): 56–58. See also Andrew H. Kydd, *Trust and Mistrust in International Relations* (Princeton, NJ: Princeton University Press, 2005).

44. Spanier and Wendzel, *Games Nations Play*, 124.

CHAPTER 7

1. Henry E. Eccles, "Strategy—Theory and Application," *Naval War College Review* 32 (May/June 1979): 13.

2. Ralph H. Gabriel, *Traditional Values in American Life* (New York: Harcourt, Brace, and World, Inc., 1963; Reprinted with permission of UNESCO) 1–32. Gabriel's work remains the start point for values.

3. Ibid., 3–5.

4. Anita M. Arms, "Strategic Culture: The American Mind," in *Essays on Strategy IX*, ed. Thomas C. Gill (Washington, DC: National Defense University Press, 1993) 12. See also pp. 3–32. For a more detailed development of these ideas and the implications for foreign policy and national style, see Roger S. Whitcomb, *The American Approach to Foreign Affairs: An Uncertain Tradition* (Westport, CT: Praeger, 1998).

5. Ibid., 12–25.

6. Donald M. Snow and Eugene Brown, *Puzzle Palaces and Foggy Bottom: U.S. Foreign and Defense Policy-Making in the 1990's* (New York: St. Martin's Press, 1994) 213–214.

7. Ibid.,. 214–215.

8. Ibid., 215–218.

9. Barry R. Posen and Andrew Ross, "Competing Visions for U.S. Grand Strategy," *International Security* 21(3) (Winter 1997): 5–53.

10. Ibid., 6, 9–15.

11. Ibid., 6, 16–22.

12. Ibid., 6, 22–31.

13. Ibid., 6, 31–43.

14. Kissinger, Henry Kissinger, *Diplomacy* (New York: Simon & Schuster, 1994) 462–463.

15. Snow and Brown, *Puzzle Palaces and Foggy Bottom*, 31–32.

16. Ibid., 32–37.

17. Ibid., 37–45.

18. Ibid., 112–119.

19. Ibid., 119–125.

20. Ibid., 117, 118, 124–125.

21. Ibid., 107–112.

22. Roger H. Davidson and Walter J. Oleszek, *Congress and Its Members* (Washington, DC: CQ Press, 2006) 3–10.

23. Ibid., 28–30.

24. David E. Sanger and Scott Shane, "Court's Ruling Is Likely to Force Negotiations Over Presidential Power," *New York Times* (Late Edition Final) (June 30, 2006).

25. Mary Jo Hatch, *Organizational Theory: Modern, Symbolic, and Post-Modern Perspectives* (New York: Oxford University Press, 1997) 210–236. See also Steven W. Hook, *U.S. Foreign Policy: The Paradox of World Power* (Washington, DC: CQ Press, 2005) 75–78.

26. Office of the Federal Register, National Archives and Records Administration, *U.S. Government Manual, 2007–2008 Edition*, GPO Access, available from

http://frwebgate.access.gpo.gov/cgi-bin/getdoc.cgi?dbname=2007_government_manual&docid=211657tx_xxx-3.pdf, accessed on September 28, 2007.

27. Vernon Loeb and Thomas E. Ricks, "Rumfeld's Style, Goals Strain Ties in Pentagon," *Washington Post* [newspaper online] October 16, 2002, A01, available from http://www.washingtonpost.com/wp-dyn/articles/A32170-2002Oct15.html, accessed on September 29, 2007.

28. Jane Perlez, "Bush Team's Counsel Is Divided on Foreign Policy," *The New York Times*, March 27, 2001. See also Thomas L. Friedman, "A Foreign Policy Built-on Do-Overs," *The New York Times*, February 23, 2007.

29. Snow and Brown, *Puzzle Palaces and Foggy Bottom*, 40–56, 70.

30. Ibid., 40–56, 70.

31. Alan Stolberg, "U.S. Army War College Interagency Briefing" (Carlisle Barracks, PA: Academic Year 2008). Used with permission, Public Domain.

32. For a history of the National Security Counsel and the various changes in names of subcommittees and practices see White House, *National Security Council* (Washington, DC), available at http://www.whitehouse.gov/nsc/history.html, accessed on September 29, 2007.

33. Stolberg, "U.S. Army War College Interagency Briefing."

34. http://clinton4.nara.gov/WH/EOP/NSC/html/NSC_Staff.html http://www.fas.org/irp/news/2005/03/nsc-reorg.pdf.

35. Stolberg, "U.S. Army War College Interagency Briefing."

36. George W. Bush, "National Presidential Directive 1: Organization of the National Security Council System," The White House, February 13, 2001; available from http://www.au.af.mil/au/awc/awcgate/whitehouse/nspd-1.htm, accessed on September 29, 2007.

37. Stolberg, "U.S. Army War College Interagency Briefing."

38. Bush, "National Presidential Directive 1."

39. Bush, "National Presidential Directive 1."

40. James Fallows, "Blind into Baghdad, *The Atlantic* 93(1) (January/February 2004): 52–74.

41. Snow and Brown, *Puzzle Palaces and Foggy Bottom*, 52–155.

42. The White House, White House Offices, available at http://www.whitehouse.gov/government/off-descrp.html, accessed on September 29, 2007.

43. The White House, Homeland Security Council Executive Order, March 19, 2002, available at http://www.whitehouse.gov/news/releases/2002/03/20020321-9.html, accessed on September 29, 2007.

44. Christopher L. Naler, "Interagency Combatant Command," DTIC, available at http://72.14.205.104/search?q=cache:mIIuClO6J8QJ:www.dtic.mil/doctrine/jel/jfq_pubs/4108.pdf+interagency+combatant+command&hl=en&ct=clnk&cd=1&gl=us, accessed on September 29, 2007.

45. The Center For the Study of the Presidency, "Project on National Security Reform," available at http://www.thepresidency.org/Leadership/pnsr.html, accessed on September 15, 2007.

46. Snow and Brown, *Puzzle Palaces and Foggy Bottom*, 193–203.

47. Ibid.

48. Ibid., 184–185.

49. Ibid., 185–203.

50. Dennis M. Simon, "The War in Vietnam 1965–1968: Americanizing the War," Southern Methodist University, available at http://faculty.smu.edu/dsimon/Change-Viet2.html, accessed on September 23, 2007.

51. Graham Allison and Philip Zelikow, *Essence of Decision: Explaining the Cuban Missile Crisis,* 2nd ed. (New York: Addison-Wesley Educational Publishers Inc., 1999) 1–11. This edition is a major revision and takes into account the new information available from both governments as well as providing enhanced explanations of the models.

52. Ibid., 13–54.

53. Ibid., 143–185.

54. Ibid., 255–313.

55. Ibid. For a detailed look at groupthink in government policy, see Irving L. Janis. *Groupthink: Psychological Studies of Policy Decisions and Fiascoes,* 2nd ed. (Boston, MA: Houghton Mifflin Company, 1982).

CHAPTER 8

1. Arthur F. Lykke, Jr., "Toward an Understanding of Military Strategy," in *Military Strategy: Theory and Application* (Carlisle Barracks, PA: U.S. Army War College, 1989) 3–8.

2. Harry R. Yarger, *Strategic Theory for the 21st Century: The Little Book on Big Strategy* (Carlisle, PA: Strategic Studies Institute, February 2006) 17–29.

3. Donald E. Nuechterlein, *America Overcommitted: United States National Interests in the 1980s* (Lexington, KY: The University Press of Kentucky, 1984) 4.

4. Joint Staff, J-7, *Joint Publication 1-02, Department of Defense Dictionary of Military and Associated Terms* (Washington, DC: United States Joint Staff, April 12, 2002; amended through September 14, 2007) 360.

5. Department of National Security and Strategy, *Course Directive: National Security Policy and Strategy Academic Year 2007* (Carlisle, PA: USAWC, 2006) 106.

6. Nuechterlein, *America Overcommitted*, 8–14.

7. *National Security Policy and Strategy Academic Year 2007*, 106–108.

8. Nuechterlein, *America Overcommitted*, 10.

9. *National Security Policy and Strategy Academic Year 2007*, 106–108.

10. Ibid., 9–14, 17–28. Nuechterlein identifies vital interests in regard to various value and cost/risk factors, discussing eight of each. These are still useful, but not inclusive.

11. Carl von Clausewitz, *On War*, ed. and trans. Michael Howard and Peter Paret (Princeton: Princeton University Press, 1976) 102.

12. *The World FactBook*, CIA, https://www.cia.gov/library/publications/the-world-factbook/print/ch.html; Internet accessed July 18, 2007.

13. George W. Bush, *The National Security Strategy of the United States of America* (Washington, DC: The White House, September 2002) 17–18.

14. George W. Bush, *The National Security Strategy of the United States of America* (Washington, DC: The White House, March 2006) 26. Here, the administration takes credit for success.

15. Clausewitz, *On War*, 102.

16. Sun-tzu, *The Art of War*, trans. Ralph D. Sawyer (New York: Barnes & Noble Books, 1994) 167.

17. Richard M. Meinhart, "Leadership and Strategic Thinking," in *Strategic Thinking* (Carlisle, PA: U.S. Army War College, 2007) 36–37.

18. Stephen J. Gerras, "Thinking Critically About Critical Thinking: A Fundamental Guide for Strategic Leaders," in *Strategic Thinking* (Carlisle, PA: U.S. Army War College, 2007) 47–75.

19. Richard E. Neustadt and Ernest R. May, *Thinking in Time: The Use of History for Decision Makers* (New York: The Free Press, 1986) 232–240, 252–256.

20. George E. Reed, "Systems Thinking and Senior Level Leadership," in *Strategic Thinking* (Carlisle, PA: U.S. Army War College, 2007) 158–162.

21. Charles D. Allen, "Creative Thinking for Individuals and Teams," in *Strategic Thinking* (Carlisle, PA: U.S. Army War College, 2007) 47–75.

22. Meinhart, "Leadership and Strategic Thinking," 44.

23. David Jablonsky, "National Power," in *U.S. Army War College Guide to National Security Policy and Strategy*, ed. J. Boone Bartholomees (Carlisle, PA: U.S. Army War College, June 2006) 127–142.

24. John Spanier and Robert L. Wendzel, *Games Nations Play*, 9th ed. (Washington, DC: Congressional Quarterly, Inc., 1996) 22–42.

25. Colin S. Gray, *Modern Strategy* (Oxford: Oxford University Press, 1999) 23–44.

CHAPTER 9

1. Williamson Murray and Mark Grimsley, "Introduction: On Strategy," in *The Making of Strategy: Rulers, States, and War* (Cambridge: Cambridge University Press, 1994, 1997) 13.

2. Robert H. Dorff, "Strategy, Grand Strategy, and the Search for Security," in *The Search for Security: A U.S. Grand Strategy for the Twenty-First Century*, ed. Max G. Manwaring, Edwin G. Corr, and Robin H. Dorff (Westport, CT: Praeger, 2003) 128–129.

3. Carl von Clausewitz, *On War*, ed. and trans. Michael Howard and Peter Paret (Princeton: Princeton University Press, 1976) 607.

4. John Lewis Gaddis, *The Landscape of History: How Historians Map the Past* (Oxford: Oxford University Press, 2002) 66.

5. Mackubin Thomas Owens, *National Review Online*, January 5, 2005; available from http://www.nationalreview.com/owens/owens200501050715.asp, accessed on January 5, 2005.

6. Russell F. Weigley, *The American Way of War: A History of United States Military Policy and Strategy* (Bloomington: Indiana University Press, 1973) 411–424.

7. Owens, *National Review Online*.

8. Robert Cooper, *The Breaking of Nations: Order and Chaos in the 21st Century* (New York: Atlantic Monthly Press, 2003) viii–xi.

CHAPTER 10

1. Colin S. Gray, *Modern Strategy* (Oxford: Oxford University Press, 1999) 2.

2. Robert Jervis, *System Effects: Complexity in Political and Social Life* (Princeton, NJ: Princeton University Press, 1997), 60.

3. Department of National Security and Strategy, *Course Directive: National Security Policy and Strategy Academic Year 2007* (Carlisle, PA: USAWC, 2006) 106–108.

CHAPTER 11

1. Gary L. Guertner, ed., *The Search for Strategy: Politics and Strategic Vision* (Westport, CT: Greenwood Press, 1993) 306.

Index

About the Author

HARRY R. YARGER is Professor of National Security Policy, U.S. Army War College. He is the author of *Strategic Theory for the 21st Century: The Little Book on Big Strategy* (USAWC, 2006); *Theory and Nature of War* (USAWC, 1997); *Strategy and Its Theorists* (USAWC, 1997). He received his Ph.D. from Temple University.

CPSIA information can be obtained
at www.ICGtesting.com
Printed in the USA
BVHW040115141120
593227BV00006B/101